*f*P

Also by Sally Helgesen

The Female Advantage: Women's Ways of Leadership
The Web of Inclusion: A New Architecture for
Building Great Organizations
Everyday Revolutionaries: Working Women and
the Transformation of American Life
Wildcatters: A Story of Texas, Oil, and Money

Thriving in
24/7

Six Strategies for Taming
the New World of Work

SALLY HELGESEN

THE FREE PRESS
New York   London   Toronto   Sydney   Singapore

THE FREE PRESS
A Division of Simon & Schuster, Inc.
1230 Avenue of the Americas
New York, NY 10020

THE FREE PRESS and colophon are trademarks
of Simon & Schuster, Inc.

For information regarding special discounts for bulk purchases,
please contact Simon & Schuster Special Sales at 1-800-456-6798
or business@simonandschuster.com

Designed by Deirdre Amthor

Manufactured in the United States of America
10 9 8 7 6 5 4 3 2 1

Library of Congress Cataloging-in-Publication Data
Helgesen, Sally, 1948–
Thriving in 24/7: six strategies for taming the new world
of work / Sally Helgesen.
p. cm.
1. Time management. 2. Work environment—Effect of
technological innovations on. 3. Quality of work life.
I. Title: Thriving in twenty-four/seven. II. Title.

HD69.T54 H458 2001
650.1—dc21
2001023723

ISBN 0-684-87303-6

For Stanley Siegel, who said to throw open the windows, crank up Puccini and have fun.

I did.

CONTENTS

ACKNOWLEDGMENTS

Thanks to Bart Gulley for his love and support, and to Elizabeth Bailey and Kathleen Cox, whose advice and encouragement pulled me through.

Thanks to my insightful and always available agent, Wes Neff; to my thoughtful and responsive editor, Rachel Klayman; and to Tom Neilssen, who understood what I was getting at enough to come up with the title. I am also grateful to Liz Maguire, who first championed the book, and to Susan Leon, whose work made it better.

Thanks finally to the many people whose voices are heard in these pages. Their generosity, their willingness to *go deep,* inspired me to believe that there are solutions to our common dilemma.

AUTHOR'S NOTE

All the people quoted in this book appear under their own names and tell their true stories. In the very few instances where people did not wish to be identified, I have told their stories without names attached, changing a few details to protect their privacy.

By the time this book was getting ready to go to press, I discovered that many people I had interviewed had changed jobs or even careers since I spoke with them in early 2000. I couldn't have asked for a more powerful demonstration of the idea at the center of this book: that we are living in a time of constant change and relentless instability.

Introduction:
New Rules for a New Game

The great challenge facing most of us today is that of trying to build satisfying and enjoyable lives in a world in which work, and even our essential daily chores, seems to require an increasing amount of time and an ever-greater intensity of attention—twenty-four hours a day, seven days a week. A world in which we frequently gear ourselves up to work in overdrive, all the while feeling that we are actually falling behind. A world in which even those blessings that should most refresh us—a long lunch with a close friend, a much-anticipated family vacation, the celebration of traditional holidays—seem at times like tasks rather than pleasures, additional items on an endless to-do list that threatens to swallow us up.

Ours is an era of unprecedented opportunity, variety, prosperity, and broadening perspectives, as we are almost continually reminded. For those of us fortunate enough to live in the flourishing "first world"—the United States, Canada, much of Europe, the more prosperous Asian and Latin countries—this is in most ways a thrilling time to be alive. This is especially true for women, who have vastly more choice and freedom than at anytime in the past, more opportunities to reinvent themselves and assume unexpected roles, more chances to pursue individual fulfillment. But it is also true for men, who have increasingly been freed from the rigid requirements of being sole breadwinner throughout the course of their adult lives. Whereas women now have greater scope to explore their public selves and potential, men have greater scope to explore their private selves and potential, greater flexibility to discover what suits them as individuals rather than feeling compelled to hunker down and sacrifice their dreams for the sake of their families.

And yet, there often seems to be a disconnect between the optimistic larger picture that confronts us and the ways in which our own particular lives are unfolding. The very technologies that were supposed to free up our time seem instead to be consuming it, tacking hours onto our already extended days. The very employers who want us to buy into their vision statements about "empowering" people in the workplace nevertheless expect us to work at an exhausting pace. The very interconnectedness of life in a global networked economy that creates so many opportunities also makes all our decisions more complex, crucial, even fraught.

As Judith Martin, "Miss Manners," has observed about our society: "The simple idea that everyone needs a reasonable amount of challenging work in his or her life, and also a personal life, complete with noncompetitive leisure, has not taken hold." Put another way, in the past, having a life while earning a living didn't seem like too much to ask. Today, even this basic goal has been redefined as "having it all."

Many of us have responded to the situation by trying to sol-

dier through. We work harder, we strive to become more organized, more efficient. We devise ambitious and demanding
schedules for ourselves, set the clock half an hour earlier each
morning, resolve to stop dawdling over lunch (or to stop eating
it!), and use the time to be more productive. And we multitask,
scanning our e-mail as we return calls, flipping through a Pow-
erPoint presentation while slogging along on the treadmill.

Yet our heroic efforts at self-discipline often have the effect
of robbing us of spontaneity and the capacity for joy, leaving us
wondering exactly what our lives are really *about*. Enjoying
downtime makes us feel guilty, but being too highly structured
and tightly scheduled makes us feel resentful, as though the
value of our lives is measured only by the ceaseless array of
duties we constantly perform.

As one bewildered woman I know expressed it, "Sometimes, I feel as if my body is just a vehicle for carrying my head
to the computer."

Clearly, this is no way to live!

So how *might* we live in today's demanding environment?
How can we best face its complex and escalating demands?
And is there a way not just to cope in our 24/7 world, but actually to *thrive* within it, to master our circumstances sufficiently
to feel as if we are the shapers of our fates? Is it possible to ful-
fill our responsibilities while also feeling fully alive, in harmony, at relative peace, *in the flow?*

I believe that it *is* possible—not easy, but achievable and
infinitely worth achieving. It is also necessary if we are to get

the most out of the rich and demanding era into which we have been born.

But I also believe that, while most of us recognize that the nature of the economy and the technologies that support it have changed radically, *we are nevertheless still trying to shape our lives according to the old rules of the industrial era.* This is the heart of our problem. This is why our best efforts are often self-defeating. This is the ultimate and true source of our frustrations. We are in an entirely new game, but we don't know how to update the rules.

We have only to consider what a typical desktop looked like in 1980 to realize how much things have changed; indeed, the very word *desktop* has a different meaning than it did twenty years ago. Fast and interactive networked technologies have quickened the pace of everything we do and expanded our individual reach exponentially. These same technologies have also had the effect of flattening hierarchies, weakening chains of command, and exposing even the greeting card shop in the nearby strip mall to global forces. As a result, organizations of every kind have grown less stable and more chaotic. This in turn has had the effect of making all of us more vulnerable, less secure in our work.

At the same time, we also have many more options that we can pursue. Talent remains at a premium. The economy fabricates jobs even in downturns. If we don't like our job, we can search for something else. And if we don't feel like assuming a prefabricated position, we can transform ourselves into an entrepreneur or solo practitioner and build a distinctive niche to call our own. We can access any market in the world directly from the desk wedged between our dining room and our kitchen. We can raise capital without ever having to call a bank. We can sell our skills back to our former employer, who may well be pleased at the prospect of outsourcing our function to us. We can join forces with our best friend from high school, or with someone we met in line at the grocery last month, and offer the world a new product or service.

Of course, there is no *guarantee* that we will succeed at our new venture. There is no assurance that taking another job or restructuring the one we have will lead to greater fulfillment. But changing our circumstances to suit our needs and desires is far easier than in the past.

Most of us understand how this fluidity and volatility affects business. We read books and articles about what it means for organizations, we attend seminars about its impact upon management. But we are not so sure what this same volatile environment means for us *as individuals,* as people struggling to build balanced, meaningful, and satisfying lives in rapidly changing and highly demanding circumstances. We are not sure what we personally need to do to adapt to the world into which we have been thrust. We do not yet know what the rules for *living* in this new economy might be.

Thriving in 24/7 is an attempt to provide some concrete answers to these common dilemmas. It aims at individuais, rather than at managers or organizations. It focuses on uncovering the new rules of the game as they affect our everyday lives, and on identifying the skills, talents, attitudes, and understandings that will best prepare us to flourish in the years ahead.

In this book, I have identified six strategies for taming the new world of work, since it is at work that we experience our environment at its most intense. I did not pluck these strategies from thin air. Rather, these strategies revealed themselves during conversations I've held over the past few years.

These conversations evolved informally, as a consequence of my work. I design and deliver seminars, workshops, and speeches for corporations, business and professional networks, and colleges and universities. My subjects include leadership, issues of workplace change, and the role of women at work. Participating in hundreds of conferences over the last decade, I have witnessed an increasing preoccupation with the issue of balance. In almost every session I have joined or led, individuals have talked about their quest for it, about the difficulties they face in achieving it, about the strategies they have developed for bringing it into their lives. They've spoken about their efforts to find meaning and fulfillment in work as a way of alleviating the pressure, about the quirks of their individual journeys, about how they have come to view their own purpose and achievements.

As a result of these dialogues, I began a series of more formal interviews with people who have found ways of fulfilling their responsibilities while achieving a real measure of satisfaction and joy in 24/7. In this book you will meet a few dozen of these people, giving voice to solutions that many others have also spoken about. I have limited the number of individuals I present both to avoid repetition and to keep the structure of the book manageable.

The people you will meet in these pages are a diverse lot: different ages, backgrounds, professions, circumstances. They approach their work in a variety of ways. They are "beyond category," as Duke Ellington used to say when asked to describe his music. But despite their differences, these people share a number of things in common:

They understand that, at some point during the mid-1990s, a fundamental shift took place in the relationship between people, time, and work.

They know that this shift has made it incumbent upon us all to abandon outdated and linear notions about what constitutes a career.

They recognize that no one-size-fits-all answer can address today's complex circumstances, that there are no more generic solutions for the simple reason that we no longer live predictable or generic lives.

They are comfortable improvising individual responses that allow scope for flexibility and enable them to remain open to continual change.

They accept that the world they are living in is different from that in which all but the very youngest among us grew up.

How can we best describe this world? Until recently many used the all-purpose term *new economy*. But I try to avoid the phrase because it can mean very different things in different contexts. Sometimes, the phrase refers to a specific segment of the economy, a particularly volatile one. At other times, it refers to how business as a whole is being altered by technological innovations. Most important, talking about the changes taking place around us in terms of the new economy

de-emphasizes their human consequence and underplays the
impact they have upon all aspects of our daily lives. For the
changes we are living through affect us in ways that go far beyond the economic realm. They are transforming our communities, our families, our personal values, our possibilities.
And these transformations are in turn helping to shape the
world that we confront at work.

I prefer to describe our 24/7 world using a phrase I first
heard while presenting a talk at the U.S. Army's senior training
college in the late 1990s. The officers I worked with had an
acronym (people in the army *always* have an acronym) to describe the world in which they were expected to function—a
world as different from that in which yesterday's army operated as can be conceived. They called this new world "VUCA"
(pronounced *voo-kah*). They were always talking about "our
VUCA environment," or describing the challenge of living "in
VUCA time."

It's not a pretty term, and at first hearing it has a kind of
hard-edged military ring. But I have come to see it as both a
useful and appropriate kind of shorthand, a good way to describe what we all face.

What does VUCA stand for?

Volatility, uncertainty, complexity, and ambiguity.

Volatility because change in this new environment is not a
onetime event, but is constantly evolving.

Uncertainty because there is no way we can predict what
might be coming next.

Complexity because each event is influenced by a chain of
interconnected events.

Ambiguity because paradoxical trends (globalization *and* a more local focus; high technology *and* more personalized, "high-touch" service) are occurring at the same time.

VUCA describes the world in which most of us have been living for the past few years. We may not yet be comfortable with this world, but we are starting to recognize that it is here to stay. We are beginning to accept that we will never return to the more static, less opportunity-rich but also more comforting world in which most of us were raised. The changes we are living through are both permanent and dynamic.

This is why we need strategies for living that take them into account.

We need such strategies especially because the era of VUCA is only now getting under way. For the speed of technological change is on the verge of a massive acceleration that will quickly gain force over the next decade. And as the Internet morphs into the evernet—turning our personal computers, electronic notebooks, PalmPilots, and wristwatches into the equivalent of perpetually open T-1 lines, primed to send and receive a constant stream of messages and information to everyone else on the planet—the institutions that we have come to know will continue to change shape, crumble, or disappear with a ferocity we can only now imagine. More instability *and* more opportunity, more dislocation *and* more choice, will be the result.

If we are to maintain a firm sense of integrity, balance, and purpose in this new world, we must begin now to master the skills and attitudes that will enable us to thrive.

In Part One of this book, we will examine the scope of the changes that affect every aspect of our existence, so we can get a clearer understanding of precisely what we are up against.

In Part Two, we will learn specific strategies that can help us tame this demanding environment and techniques for putting these strategies into practice.

We are moving into unmapped territory now, an exciting yet daunting geography. This book is intended as a guide to help us navigate what we find as we go.

PART ONE

The Challenge of Living in 24/7

The real consequence of emerging science and technology is not gadgets, whether hydrogen bombs or silicon chips, but radical social change; ever-increasing diversity and complexity in the way people live and work.

Dee Hock
Founder, VISA International

1

When Work Invades Life

The most obvious challenge of life in VUCA is the extent to which work has infringed upon our lives. At times it seems as if this is simply part of the landscape, a given to which we must somehow adjust. When Federal Express, in June 1999, introduced Sunday delivery, the banner advertising the new service proclaimed "For the Way the World Works Now."

And indeed, it *is* more and more the way the world works, at least in the United States and in those cities—London, Tokyo, Vancouver, Hong Kong, Brussels, Bangalore—that have become the nerve centers of our global business culture. It's a world of midnight arrivals at Heathrow or O'Hare, where we are greeted by Ericsson Communications ads reminding us to "Call the office, even if it's here," or to "Kiss the kids good night—whether they're around the corner or around the world." It's a world where Kinko's is never closed and never empty, a world in which we call our mortgage broker or our teenage niece and get a voice mail with beeper and cell-phone numbers along with an e-mail address and the assurance that she need never be out of touch.

It's a world in which the planners of a corporate or association retreat held over the weekend (a dubious notion in itself) can with a straight face offer a seminar called "Achieving Balance" at seven A.M. on a Sunday morning (I've been at such retreats, I've seen it done).

This world has crept up on us over the last twenty years or so, confounding many of our expectations. After all, it was only thirty-five years ago that the U.S. Congress recommended the permanent institution of a cabinet-level Office on Hobbies to help society deal with the oceans of leisure time that everyone presumed would result from the introduction of computer-based technologies in the final decades of the twentieth century! This new world (from which, on the contrary, leisure often seems to be nearly absent) has transformed our relationship to time and work so entirely that many of us have come to accept our harried pace as part of the landscape, *the way things are.*

Until recently, the problem of finding alignment or balance between work and life was often viewed as a "women's issue," since women were the first to be faced with the challenge of bearing a full load at work while also performing a broad range of duties at home. Women were thus caught in the ensuing crunch, which the sociologist Arlie Hochschild famously dubbed the "second shift." But by the late 1990s, things began to change. Men also could be heard lamenting that work was swallowing up an impossible amount of their time, an onerous situation since they were now being asked to assume more responsibility at home. As a result, human resources executives found themselves dealing with mounting dissatisfaction from both men and women. A recent Gallup poll found that *fully 40 percent* of Americans described themselves as feeling anywhere from "somewhat angry" to "very angry" while on the job, their key complaints being too much work and technology overload.

What is going on?

By rights, this should be a great time for people at work, and by many measures it is. The labor market has been tight for years, and almost everyone with marketable skills has flourished financially. The growing premium placed on knowledge in the marketplace, and the emphasis on innovation, flexibility, and creativity, has made organizations more dependent than ever on their people. In a neat reversal of Marxist ideology, we now find ourselves living in a capitalist economy in which we as workers own the primary means of production. Those means of production—our ideas, our thoughts, our very brains—are lodged in our heads and get into the elevator with us when we leave for home each night. This gives us a level of power we may not have recognized or accepted.

As a result of the increasing value placed on human talent, companies have been tripping over themselves in the last few years to put out vision and mission statements proclaiming how much they care about their people. Competition to be named one of "America's Best Companies to Work For" has grown fierce, and other nations have begun to compile their own rankings. The bad old days, when a CEO like Bob Crandall of American Airlines blamed flight attendants for the company's financial slump, or when "Chainsaw Al" Dunlop gained fame (and, in many quarters, *respect*) for performing serial firings of employees at a succession of companies—those days are clearly on the wane.

· · ·

Given the need organizations have for good people, we might have anticipated that the number of hours we are expected to work would drop, since our bargaining power should increase with our rising value in the marketplace. And indeed, economists have long predicted that work hours are about to to fall, as they have in the past whenever labor markets have tightened.

Yet this has failed to happen, and conversation in the workplace has remained centered on issues of burnout and stress, with people one-upping each others' tales of marathon efforts and frequent flier miles earned on the job. Even companies that *want* to reverse the trend toward longer hours have found themselves powerless to do so. Every technological advancement requires another round of training; intense competition makes instant response to client and customer demands essential. As a result, the most enlightened employers have found it difficult to practice the "human-centered" policies they not only profess to champion but also know are in their best long-term interest.

What is the source of this contradiction? There are several causes.

To begin with, most companies have spent the better part of the last decade getting leaner—downsizing, rightsizing, whatever they choose to call it. Productivity has soared as a result. But *people* in the workplace have paid a price. Those who have remained in their jobs have found themselves taking up slack for those who have left. Those who have left have joined companies that are also leaner.

At the same time, key networked technologies have become dramatically more pervasive, putting fresh demands upon our time and invading our most private spaces. I recall in 1999 listening as a woman called her office *while taking a shower* in the health club of the Oakbrook Marriott, a popular conference hotel outside Chicago. Another woman I spoke with, who had recently stayed up all night finishing a report her boss needed for an early client meeting, ended up downloading her ten-year-old's book report by mistake and e-mailing it to the client; meanwhile, she zipped the report she had written into the child's backpack and sent her off to school. Everyone these days has similarly ludicrous stories.

And so the last decade has been a time of comedy, brilliance, paradox, hope, breakthrough, pressure, and mistake—a time when some things have gotten better in the workplace, but many people have felt worse because of overwork. Companies have hardly been unaware of the contradiction. One senior manager at Johnson & Johnson described the situation to me succinctly: "My biggest problem these days is that my people have become increasingly skeptical of me and resentful about the demands I am forced to make. I trace this directly to the fact that there's just so much pressure, so much work, that we're operating more leanly than we used to, and that we're really getting seriously global. So I'm always having to tell my people, okay, *this* job is going to require a major effort, we're going to have to give 120 percent for the next two weeks, but then it will be done and we can all relax a little. So everyone gives that 120 percent, but as soon as that project is over, I have to tell them the exact same thing about the next job. It's not even the *amount* of work that's the problem so much as the fact that the *pace* is unrelenting; as soon as people have gotten through one thing, there's something else on the horizon. So everyone gets turned off because they're sick of the constant sacrifice. And, of course, the best people leave."

And this at Johnson & Johnson, named in the *Wall Street Journal* as the most admired company in America! Organizations have responded to the problem in various ways. Some have instituted Work and Family programs, usually run by the Human Resources department, that struggle nobly to develop policies and procedures that allow employees the option of flexible hours, and make allowances for specific circumstances (the adoption of a child, a spouse's continuing illness) while also trying *somehow* to treat all employees as equal. Others have initiated elaborate retention efforts, aimed at convincing employees how deeply they are valued, and creating various perks to boost morale. Recognition Day, team retreats at appealing resorts, access to high-level mentors, a full array of citations and awards have become standard features in many organizations.

Yet other companies have dramatically increased the financial incentives they offer, from company-financed low-rate mortgages to escalating stock options to luxury items. The purpose of such incentives is often to persuade people to stay on the job despite dissatisfaction with working hours, as in the well-publicized instance of the hard-charging Virginia software firm that promised to lease a BMW for any employee who stayed with the company at least two years!

Taken together, these efforts have not been an unqualified success, at least according to the business press: "Lawyers Dropping Out in Unprecedented Numbers," headlines the *New York Times;* "Women Still Opting Out of the Rat Race," declares *Fortune;* "The Talent Drought: Is There an End in Sight?" worries *Business Week.* But the amount of money being thrown at retention programs indicates how intractable (and how troublesome for the corporate brass) the challenge of retaining good people has become in today's all-work-all-the-time organizational culture.

The basic problem is that few of the initiatives meant to deal with the problem have questioned the root and basis of this culture, or analyzed what is really happening and why. Organizations tend to assume that people will sacrifice time if they are paid enough money, that this trade-off is acceptable for most. Employees, on the other hand, know what their companies are up against in terms of competition, and are eager to show that they are entrepreneurial self-starters, willing to sacrifice to achieve the mission. And in an era when the team is held in highest esteem, people hesitate to ask "*Why* does this report have to be in tomorrow?" for fear that they will be branded a poor team player—the worst of fates in today's workplace.

Clearly, we've worked ourselves into a fix.

To address this bind with imagination and power and find solutions that meet our individual needs, we must first understand exactly how a convergence of changes—*occurring at the same time and thus compounding one another's effects*—has transformed the world in which all of us work. For it is this convergence that has created the environment of pressure and instability that drags us down.

The confluence of changes includes the following:

A new architecture of technology

Until recently, most of us just assumed that our growing use of fast, interactive technologies would at some point free up great portions of our time. Instead, the plethora of new devices has enabled us to accomplish more things within the scope of a single day or week. Thus our cell phones, laptops, PalmPilots, and modems have had the ultimate effect of raising our expectations (and those of our employers) about how much we might reasonably achieve.

In retrospect, our assumptions were naive. Throughout history, new technologies have had similar results. The invention of the washing machine did not mean that less time was spent doing laundry, but rather that people came to expect much cleaner clothes. The development of the tractor did not lessen the time a farmer labored in his fields, but rather enabled him to cultivate far more land. In the same way, e-mail has not cut down on the time most of us devote to correspondence, but has instead made it possible to correspond on a regular (or daily, or even hourly) basis with far greater numbers of people. Even the spread of automatic teller machines did not really reduce the amount of time we spend on our banking, but rather enticed most of us to replace our twice-a-month regime of withdrawals with constant stops whenever we find ourselves in need of cash.

This constant raising of expectations and standards is an aspect of all technological advancement, but the very *architecture* of today's technologies intensifies these effects. Microchip-based tools are unique in that they become smaller, more powerful, and cheaper with every passing year, which means that their use spreads rapidly. As a result, they permit and encourage short product cycles, which in turn require companies to work harder just to stay in place. These rapid cycles also compel those of us who use these products to continually update our skills, for no sooner have we mastered the latest up-grade of our software than the new version sweeps into the market.

And so digital technologies, operating at speeds beyond human consciousness, are dramatically altering the nature of our world and doing so at an increasingly rapid pace. We human beings, however, remain essentially the same creatures we have been for the last twenty thousand years, evolution being notoriously slow. This disjunction between the environment we are creating and our own essential selves destabilizes us at every turn. To really keep up with the tools we use, we would have to become *more like them*—exponentially faster, more interconnected, and more information-rich.

Since creation will always outrun adaptation, this is never going to happen. And so the pace of digital development is literally *programmed* to exhaust us. We can work harder, faster, and longer; we can push ourselves to the utmost point of endurance; but we will *still* fall behind as the pace of technological change continues to quicken. Because we cannot even hope to keep up, we have no choice but to adjust our priorities and expectations.

The ascent of knowledge

The present shift from an industrial economy based upon the manufacture of heavy equipment to a knowledge economy based on ideas and innovation has also made work far more invasive. To begin with, competition in a knowledge economy *can come from anywhere*. Large amounts of capital are simply not as valuable or important as a great idea itching to be born. This fact lies behind the extraordinary entrepreneurial boom that has taken place over the last decade, undermining hierarchies and freeing individuals from organizational control as never before.

But the value of knowledge also requires companies and entrepreneurs to work harder and faster than in the past, because decades of work can be wiped out overnight by a competitor with few resources. Microsoft was able to overtake IBM with a minimal investment; early technology powerhouses such as Digital Equipment and Wang disappeared because they bet on the wrong kind of technology; *the* original networking company, AT&T, continues to struggle. Thus, when our company tells us that there's no room for slacking because the environment punishes laggards, they are telling the truth—and we know it.

In addition, the primary tools we use to do knowledge work are small and portable. This has had the effect of decentralizing work, enabling it to be done anytime, anywhere—a situation that is naturally invasive. This is the precise opposite of what occurred in the industrial era, when the tools of work (huge looms, vast mechanical engines, massive plants) became constantly larger and more expensive, requiring those who worked with them to travel to where they were installed. Indeed, we are living in greater intimacy with our work today than people have since the pre-industrial era, when most work was done on the farm, at the manor house, or in the cottage. In that world, however, long-standing traditions and religious observance, often tied to the changing of the seasons, as well as the impossibility of working after dark, prevented work from taking over people's lives. None of these barriers protect us today.

Finally, just being in transition from one kind of economy to another increases the amount of work that we must do. The instability caused by the transition means that we frequently change jobs—a time-consuming task that also requires enormous mental and emotional effort. And because we are in transition, we have not yet put into place appropriate safeguards to buffer us from a culture of overwork. In the industrial economy, work was kept within bounds by a broad consensus on the desirability of a "family wage," by national policies mandating a forty-hour workweek (in much of Europe, thirty-five), and by the collective bargaining of organized labor. But these institutions and practices have proven too broad and generic, too focused on maintaining the status quo, to be relevant in today's flexible knowledge economy, and have thus grown weaker in recent years. However, we have not yet established new infrastructures of support to protect us from the invasion of work. This will be our task in years to come.

Global reach

More powerful and cheaper communications, as well as a decade of wide-ranging trade agreements, have enabled more of us to do business with more of the world. Yet until we find a way to erase the differences between time zones (someone is no doubt working on it), increasing numbers of us will have to stretch our hours to keep up.

Investment bankers, at the mercy of international trading exchanges, have long had to field 2 A.M. calls from Tokyo, then set the alarm again for five to get an update from London. But now law, accounting, and consulting firms are also going global, as are corporations and independent contractors of every kind. Hospitals and medical specialists routinely keep in touch, with research taking place in every corner of the planet. Publishers report to media conglomerates half a world away, journalists report from war zones via satellite, and archaeologists compare findings from digs taking place simultaneously in Chile and China. Thus, more of us find ourselves doing work that requires us to operate across time zones, obliterating the predictable world of nine to five.

The globalizing of the market, along with the lowering of airline fares that followed deregulation throughout the world, has also created a pervasive culture of business travel, which improvements in videoconferencing seem powerless to alter. While working on a previous book that contrasted the lives of professionals in a contemporary American suburb with their counterparts in the 1950s, I was struck by how small a role business travel played in the lives of mid–twentieth century achievers. Airport proximity was not an issue, most clients were nearby, and those far away simply waited for a response. Off-site retreats were almost unheard of.

Today, by contrast, fully 30 percent of those occupying management positions in Fortune 1000 companies travel for business at least once a week, and many thousands of us log more than a quarter million miles a year. Often, the escalating demands of travel have crept up on us. One project director at a New York–based architectural firm felt weighed down five years ago because her job required her to spend two days every week in Chicago. Now she's out of town three days a week, but her commute is to Brussels. Only the most senior executives, those with access to private planes, traveled this way fifteen years ago; now many managers, salespeople, and consultants do. The exponential growth of work-related air travel (which is expected to produce gridlock in the world's airports within the decade) has played a major role in work consuming an ever-greater portion of our lives.

The breakdown of traditional barriers

In the industrial era, men ruled over the worlds of enterprise, politics, and money, while women's domain was the kitchen, the garden, and the nursery. This scheme presented many drawbacks and enforced great inequities, but the division of labor also proved quite efficient. Now the concerns of work and home are integrated, the province of both men and women, and are open for negotiation at every turn. Whereas home once served as a refuge from work, it's now more like a branch office.

As the barriers between work and home lose their sharp definition, so do those boundaries that once divided the public and private spheres of life. What most people previously regarded as their private business—divorce, child support, medical choices, sexual behavior, child care solutions, even workplace banter—has become matter for public debate and national policy. At the same time, public decisions about issues such as health care coverage and school vouchers today shape our personal lives and engage our private passions. We also use the technologies of work to organize our personal business, which invests it with a more worklike character.

Finally, because of the increasing prevalence of stock options, employee ownership programs, "intrapreneuring" units, and flat organizational styles, the old separations between boss and employee, manager and owner, are also eroding. This gives us more responsibility at work, but without the authority that bosses and owners have to set their own schedules. The walls between organizations are also growing more porous, as companies (as well as universities and nonprofits, government agencies and military organizations) form closer relationships with vendors, clients, and competitors. This requires those of us who work for these companies to be in contact with greater numbers of people, and blurs the lines that determine who can ask what from us. The trend is reflected in our private lives as well, as personal and work-life networks overlap, breaching boundaries between who is a friend and who is a "contact." All this breaking down of barriers presents many advantages, but also has the effect of creating more work.

More responsibility, less support

Work is also invading our lives because more of us are likely to be in fields or professions that are highly demanding in terms both of hours and focus. People whose professions have grown most rapidly during the last two decades—investment bankers, corporate lawyers, accountants, consultants, medical residents—have traditionally worked from sixty to eighty hours a week because the nature of such work is driven by crisis and deadline. There has also been an explosion of web-based workers, software designers, and engineers, whose culture from the start has glorified the all-nighter, the crazed genius who lives in his office consuming junk food.

In addition, pressure to work long hours has always been strongest among those who earn salaries rather than wages, those who have a direct financial stake in their company, and those who are self-employed. These categories have all grown rapidly over the last two decades. Finally, the flattening of hierarchies throughout organizations has required those who are managers to manage ever larger numbers of people.

The decline of support staff has played a huge part in work taking up more time. Until the very recent past, organizations routinely employed secretaries, supervisors, and a whole range of assistants whose job it was to handle specialized work. Even the smallest venture had a receptionist posted at the front door. This is no longer the case. New technologies have created a do-it-yourself workplace culture, in which virtually all of us assume an unprecedented variety of tasks that used to be somebody else's (or our own) exclusive job. We photocopy our reports, design our presentations, order office supplies online, use the Internet to do research, handle our filing, answer our correspondence, and return our own calls. Organizations are fond of boasting about how efficiently they outsource work, but those are the big jobs. When it comes to the details, we all sweat them.

The portable and omnipresent office

Today priority is given in every possible setting to people who are working. Hotels advertise the number of ports and phone links available in each room, the personal fax machines, the broadband lines that will (presumably) enable us to connect to the Internet even while we sleep. Vacation retreats that draw us because of their remote location and promise of privacy nevertheless offer business centers and conference rooms so we can keep working while getting away from it all. Planes and trains provide in-seat phones and plugs for our PCs, so we needn't "waste" a single moment. Satellite access is coming soon to business class.

While all this is convenient, it also creates difficulties for anyone who does *not* feel like working every minute of the day. Reading a novel or taking a nap while flying from Chicago to Denver becomes a guilty if not impossible pleasure when we are crammed in next to someone making sales calls or pounding on a laptop. The old meditative atmosphere that used to enfold commuters taking an early morning train—people dozing over their newspapers, staring out the window at the dawn, silently contemplating the day ahead—has been replaced by a frenzy of work that anticipates and mimics the office. Even at a good restaurant, we find ourselves surrounded by diners lugging around the paraphernalia of their professional lives.

The message of all this is that we *should* be using our spare moments to work, that we are slackers if we do not, that we are more deserving of consideration when we are working than when we are not. Thus, work is elevated by our daily environment into something that is appropriately done everywhere and at every conceivable moment.

•   •   •

The confluence of these six changes has dramatically accelerated a process that has been taking place since the start of the industrial revolution: the distortion of our human experience of time. As the sociologist Eviatar Zerubavel points out in his fascinating book *Hidden Rhythms,* people experience time in two very different ways: as the cyclical rhythms of nature, governed by the recurrent seasons, and as the repetitive rhythms of the machine, regulated by schedules and clocks.

If we take Zerubavel's insight and apply it to what has happened to most of us in regard to time, a disturbing progression becomes apparent. We see that in the agricultural era, people worked *and* lived in accord with cyclical rhythms. These rhythms governed every aspect of life: the procurement of necessities, relationships within the extended family, the running of the household, religious festivals and celebrations. They reflected the ancient wisdom of the Psalm, that to everything there is a season.

With the coming of the industrial age, the rhythms of the machine began to shape work that was done outside the home in order for the family to earn enough to live. People in factories and later offices performed repetitive actions without any reference to the season. They worked "against" the clock, according to a schedule whose only imperative was economic. They thus left the rhythms of nature behind.

Yet through it all, the home and garden remained places of sanctuary, governed by cyclical time, where most activities took place in accord with the seasons. Holidays were celebrated on recurrent days, children learned in winter and played or helped out in summer, household chores ranging from spring cleaning to the canning of fruit took place at the same time every year. And so while most men (with the exception of farmers) worked in accord with mechanical time, women, sequestered at home, honored and lived by timeless seasonal rhythms. The separation, not only of work and home, but also of how time was measured in the two domains, had the effect of devaluing women's economic standing within the family. But it did ensure that the private life of the family was governed by a sense of time based in nature.

With the entrance of large numbers of women into the workforce, this sequestering of private life has become a rarity. Machine time—linear, repetitive, governed by the clock—now rules the home as well as the workplace. With both parents working, the household must increasingly be run in accord with clock-based schedules. Everyone's day and week must be prearranged, so that varying timetables can be accommodated.

And so laser-printed calendars detailing precisely who does what and when have become common features on refrigerator doors. Holiday celebrations are scaled back or catered, or the family goes away for a ski vacation. The garden has become a luxury, a place to grow flowers rather than an integral aspect of household economy. All this has the effect of freeing those women who did not enjoy canning beans, drying herbs, or baking pies. It has also given men a partner who can share the economic burden. Nevertheless, one end result is that the home is no longer a refuge from workplace rhythms.

In addition, over the last decade, microchip technologies have vastly speeded up the rate at which mechanical time is gauged. As a result, every aspect of our lives is now governed by measures that operate at a speed *fundamentally out of sync with human nature.* Cut free from the old cyclical rhythms that have always been part of the human experience, we recognize that something essential has been lost, although we cannot precisely name it. So we simply observe that "no one has any time anymore," and lament our feeling of always being rushed.

Yet our protests betray our recognition that we have created a world in which an essential aspect of our humanity has little chance of finding expression. For our ancient relationship to recurrent time and the seasons—our deep embeddedness within it—has been undermined by the demands that shape our lives.

This, even more than our long working hours, is the underlying reason for our feeling that work has invaded what used to be our lives. This is why we often find ourselves unable to relax when we do get some free time, why we reach for the cell phone to fill an "empty" moment, why frequent airline travel is so enervating. We are uneasy because the world we have made for ourselves does not reflect the breadth and depth of who we are. It is not simply that time is getting away from us, or that work intrudes on our leisure. *We have also forfeited ways of being that are fundamental to us as humans.* We have undermined the relationship with time that provided our basic link to nature.

In Europe, food that has been genetically engineered is widely referred to as "frankenfood." Like Frankenstein's monster, such food is seen as a highly artificial creation, unconnected to the naturally evolving world. By eating it, we feed ourselves with the products of our own estrangement. In a similar vein, work that enables us to earn a living (even a great living) but also consumes us and destroys our capacity to live our lives fully and joyously might be described as "frankenwork."

2

When Life Itself Becomes Incredibly Complex

Most of us recognize the extent to which our lives are being consumed by work. Agonizing about it has become part of the global conversation. What is less recognized is the extent to which our private lives and even our leisure also require a lot more work these days. Simply meeting the normal responsibilities of adulthood (*forget* having to earn a living) has become something of a high-wire act. This is the perplexing reality, even the dirty little secret, of contemporary life: that we are exhausting ourselves not just at work, but also at home.

More and more, we find ourselves bringing professional-level skills and tools (PCs, Filofaxes, beepers) into the management of our domestic lives. More and more, we find our personal to-do lists getting the better of us. Arranging a sit-down dinner with the whole family at midweek can involve coordinating five different schedules. Planning a family vacation can be as challenging as holding a meeting of team members from different office locales. Simply trying to see an old friend for coffee can result in a frustrating game of phone tag or a flood of e-mails.

33

And because our private schedules are packed and precari-
ous, ruled by multiple pickups, drop-offs, by children's lessons
and personal appointments, we get little relief from the constant pressure. If something unexpected occurs—if the dog
gets sick, if the babysitter quits—our precisely choreographed
plans can be thrown into disarray. The need to attend to so
many details can also distract us from the larger picture. One
man related how he and his wife packed up the whole family
for a trip, set the house alarms, dropped off the cat and the dog
at their respective sitters, drove to the airport, checked six bags,
parked in the long-term lot and took a van back, only to discover at the gate that their flight was scheduled for the following day. They had been so caught up with the intricacies of
their plans they had forgotten to look at the calendar, or the
tickets.

We all have similar stories. Why?

Our dilemma is that the same forces that have created a
more intense and demanding workplace—the breakdown of
traditional boundaries, the rapid spread of networked technologies, faster product cycles, higher expectations—are also
transforming our lives at home. At the same time, our domestic lives reflect the major trend that dominates the consumer
marketplace today: an ever-increasing emphasis on variety
and choice. This requires us to make a constant stream of decisions about everything from the ground rules of our marriage to the age at which we have our children to how we
exercise. The fact that life at home *and* at work now demands
more energy and attention can leave us feeling as if there is no
escape.

One difficulty (which is in many ways also a blessing) is

that ours has become the great "have it your way" society. The incredible range of options we confront enables us to tailor both our activities and our purchases to meet highly specific needs and wants. In my last book, I referred to this as the Starbucks Syndrome of Contemporary Life, for whereas it used to be enough simply to ask for a "coffee to go," we now stand in two different lines to place our order for a "tall double decaf skinny latte with flat foam and a shot and a half of almond syrup"—or whatever highly personalized choice suits our individual taste. The same principle applies to almost every aspect of our lives. There is so much available that we are constantly forced to customize our selections, big and small.

Because we have so many options, there are no typical or generic patterns anymore, no "average way of life" we can just slot into without having to give it a lot of thought. At home as well as at work, we find ourselves inventing our lives as we go along, improvising in an effort to take advantage of the bewildering range of choices that we face. Our situation offers tremendous opportunities for individual fulfillment and self-expression, and keeps the economy humming along. But it also requires that we expend a great deal of energy making what were until recently fairly routine and straightforward decisions. And so we have a richer environment today, but a far more daunting one as well.

The convergence of intensity at home and at work requires us to seek new solutions. But before we can identify them, we need a clear understanding of the many ways in which our domestic lives have been transformed over the last two decades.

Our finances

We have tremendous choice in how to handle our finances today. Millions of us have become investors during the last ten
years, and substantial numbers of us manage our own money.
We have multiple checkbooks and online brokers, we move in
and out of mutual funds, and we transfer our earnings into retirement accounts. Faced with so many choices (more than
sixty thousand stock funds alone!), we try to educate ourselves
by reading financial magazines and investment newsletters, or
log onto the Motley Fool website to learn what real people say
about various companies. We have an average of six credit
cards, and pay a far greater number of monthly bills than people did in the past. And if ours is among the twenty-four million households carrying credit card debt, we routinely transfer
balances to new accounts that offer low introductory rates and
then transfer our debt again when the time is up.

The result of all this is that we have far more opportunities
to make (and lose) money on our own than people did in the
past. This is for the most part all to the good, and few of us
would want to return to an era when four percent interest was
the rule and only the rich had the opportunity to participate in
the market. But managing our money today requires a great
deal of research and information, as well as the constant making of nerve-wracking decisions. Those of us busy with jobs
and families still feel we must keep an eye on Federal Reserve
announcements and the state of various economies overseas.
We dutifully monitor inflation indexes that might affect our in-
vestments or indicate it's the right moment to refinance our
home. All this consumes a great deal of time and emotion. The

rewards can be substantial, but we need to recognize that we are also paying a price. And to know that it is *unprecedented* for large numbers of people to devote so much time to managing, and trying to grow or just preserve, their wealth.

Our health

Health care has become one of the most intricate and demanding aspects of our lives over the last two decades. Even those among us whose companies still provide a full range of health benefits are likely to have gone through major shifts, often several times. Employers will likely have changed insurers, whereas the insurers themselves may have merged, been acquired, or spun off, with the result that policies are continually revised. We may find a whole set of doctors whom we like, then be obliged to leave them and find others because our insurer devises a new set of standards. We may be required to visit a primary-care provider before we are approved to seek specialized help. We may have our claims questioned or denied, putting the burden upon us to supply particular documentation and make an absurd number of querulous phone calls. And of course, those of us who are self-employed, employed by small companies, or employed part-time must exert continual vigilance in the hunt for affordable plans.

We also know more now about chronic illnesses than people did in the past, and so we assume greater responsibility for taking care of ourselves. We experiment with special diets to manage our blood pressure or menstrual upsets, to offset a family history of heart disease, depression, or a particularly dreaded form of cancer. We exercise because we know the role it plays in keeping us healthy in body, mind, and spirit.

But we don't just jump on a bike or go for a swim; instead, we take a more comprehensive and scientific approach, balancing aerobics (calibrated to achieve the desired heart rate) with routines that develop strength and increase flexibility. We don't simply swallow a daily vitamin but count out and consume at precise times an array of specialized supplements, adding new ones as discoveries are made and advisories issued. Certainly, our efforts at self-improvement enhance our lives and keep us more youthful than previous generations, but they also burden us with a fresh array of tasks.

Our children

Raising children is a source of great joy, but the nature of parenting has changed in the last few decades, becoming far more complex and requiring an almost professional level of involvement. Not long ago, kids routinely attended the local school and spent their time afterward riding bikes around the neighborhood, perhaps attending a nearby scouting camp in the summer. Curriculum choices at school were fairly limited, as were extracurricular activities. When the time came for college, teenagers filled out an average of three applications, six pages each.

Today, there are specialized schools, charter schools, magnet schools, professional schools, and local schools with special programs—the number and variety of which increase each year. Most require vigorous testing and multiple evaluations before a student is admitted, even to kindergarten. Starting in middle school, children choose from a wide range of courses. During the summer, if families have the means, children attend tennis camps, gymnastics camps, art camps, computer camps, often several in two-week sequences. After school, they take a wide range of lessons. Kids' soccer games—even soccer *practices*—have become major social events, requiring snacks and supporters and transportation.

As a result, even young children have schedules: play dates with friends, standing dates with tutors, sessions with private coaches. They may have been diagnosed as being gifted, having ADHD, or being oppositional-defiant, in which case they are seen by counselors and therapists, who may suggest medications that need to be monitored daily. Their applications for college run to scores of pages, and they often apply to as many as twelve schools because gaining entrance has become so competitive. Parents worried about getting their children into college often start marketing them when they are young, creating desirable "packages" or brands: the figure skater, the violin prodigy, the tech whiz, the junior entrepreneur.

All this presents many advantages for today's children, offering them a richness of exposure and opportunity that only the most privileged youngsters enjoyed in the past. Still, no one could argue that it has made parenthood any simpler. The emphasis on variety, options, and competition that pervades our lives as adults also characterizes the lives of our children. This requires us to make a continual investment of time, attention, and high stakes decision-making, along with doing an unprecedented amount of driving and filling out of forms.

The sociologist Dolores Hayden has noted that "Americans

at the end of the millennium have evolved the most labor-intensive style of parenting ever known to the human race"—a style that is spreading fast to other prosperous parts of the world. That we have adopted this style *at the same time* that many of us are overwhelmed by our work—and in a period when both parents usually work—goes a long way to explaining the pressure we are under.

Our vehicles

Since 1990, there have been more cars registered in the United States than there are licensed drivers, and the disproportion of cars to drivers increases every year. In addition to basic family transport, one of the adults in a two-parent household may have a smaller car that he or she drives, while teenagers who attend different schools (or the same school, but have different after-school activities) are likely to drive their own cars as well. Perhaps the family also has a 4X4 for weekends, a snowmobile for winter sports, or a camper for long vacations. Boat ownership has dramatically increased, up more than 300 percent in the last twenty years, while the number of personal watercraft such as jet skis has gone through the roof. In upscale, though hardly wealthy suburbs, three-car garages are now the norm.

More freedom, more independence, more fun, no doubt, but all these vehicles also require a lot more maintenance and record-keeping. In addition, the glut of cars means that we sit in traffic longer: The amount of time we spend in traffic has increased more than 200 percent since 1984. We make more trips to the repair shop, pay a greater number of insurance premiums, spend more time deciding what to buy and shopping for bargains. And of course, most vehicles now come with a daunting range of options for us to choose among—from cold weather packages to global-positioning units—requiring still more decisions, maintenance, and research.

Our travel habits

Lower airline costs and pervasive business travel have made us much more casual about jumping onto planes than people were in the past. Average household air miles have increased enormously in the last twenty years. Millions of us take cruises, tour national parks, go to Florida or the islands during the winter, try to take the kids to every major theme park. We also routinely extend or add onto our business trips, inviting husbands to join us in Tucson after we conclude a corporate retreat or wives to meet us in Boston during a conference. Our travel habits have made us more cosmopolitan and better informed, but they have also made our lives far more difficult to manage than in the days when a family vacation simply meant jumping into the car to visit the grandparents.

We keep folders on cities we might visit, download highway directions, total points from rental-car agencies and chain hotels, track our frequent flyer miles and redeem them via automated systems, fight the mobs at airports, cope with massive delays and disruptions at holiday time, and keep going back for more. We buy digital cameras and camcorders to document our journeys, then beam the results to relatives via cyberspace. We join travel clubs or buy part-time shares in

vacation condos. And increasingly, we bypass our local travel
agents for help with our plans, going instead to cyberauction
sites for the best deals, the cheapest tickets, the most interesting locales.

Travel has also increasingly become a source of self-improvement rather than just a way to relax. We sign up for
wine tours of France that include lectures and tastings in various regions, or take cooking classes in Tuscany. We tour the
great museums in a group guided by an art historian, visit the
markets of northern Thailand with a textile expert, explore
the monarch butterfly breeding ground in central Mexico. Or
we test the limits of our endurance with adventure travel, a
fast-growing holiday trend. We climb Machu Picchu (millions of people did last year), raft down the Snake River in
whitewater season (forty-seven adventure companies offer
versions of this trip), try slickrock biking in southern Utah,
sign up for scuba-diving classes in the Caymans. Most of
these adventures require us to purchase special gear and
equipment, learn new skills, get into training, do research,
reread our insurance policies. More and more, travel today is
apt to be exciting, challenging, and ambitious, thus requiring
a high degree of organization and commitment and—let's
face it—*work*.

Our basic services

Deregulation has changed what used to be a fairly straightforward relationship with the phone or electric company into a
time-consuming and intricate affair. We now buy customized

services from a range of competing companies and resellers. We purchase local and long distance from different vendors, choose options ranging from call-waiting to ten-cent Sunday dialing, and put them together in packages whose costs we calibrate and negotiate in advance. We change these packages as well as our providers when we are offered a new deal, when the companies merge, or to take advantage of mileage or credit card offers and discounted rates. We have extra lines for home faxes, modems, or children's telephones, and we buy service and maintenance contracts for them all. Various family members have phone cards from different sources. When we make a long-distance call, we press up to thirty-four digits to access our account, doing work the operator used to perform.

Cable television is on our list of basic services, and here too we have an ever-increasing number of packages to choose from, which we may change as new channels are added. Most middle-class families have at least one Internet service provider, one or more e-mail accounts per family member, as well as several cell phone accounts, all of which we select from a bewildering array of options. We split electric and fuel bills among competing vendors. We pay a raft of monthly bills for these services, monitor them closely, and change them every time we move. When we need to make inquiries, we thread our way through an irritating series of automated prompts. Thus do the services we consume at home fill our days with innumerable little chores that require us to interact with networked machines, just as we do at work. Again, we have more choices, more opportunities, a richer environment, but one that requires a high degree of organization and constant attention.

Our stuff

Most of us today seek out highly specific items that meet our specialized needs when we shop. We don't dash out and buy a pair of sneakers; we purchase athletic shoes to fit particular activities, such as running, aerobics, cross-training, tennis, and biking. We search out a different bagel flavor to satisfy each member of the family. If we subscribe to a decorating magazine, we select something tailored to our needs—first apartment, contemporary luxury condo, country cottage, restored Victorian, or maybe a magazine entirely devoted to the kitchen or the bath. If we buy sheets, we pay attention to the thread count and whether it will fit our mattress (is it *deep* enough?). Even an item as mundane as dental floss comes in thirty-six varieties!

All this customizing and emphasis on choice can be gratifying—it's nice to have our individual needs catered to, to choose from among relaxed, reverse, straight-legged, lean, or classic fit when we buy a pair of Gap jeans. But it also requires us to spend an enormous amount of time analyzing and procuring even the most basic goods. With multiple products vying for limited shelf space, whatever we ultimately decide on is apt to be out of stock. In addition, the sheer *volume* of goods available requires that they be sold in ever-larger spaces, which means bigger stores with bigger parking lots, often in distant locations. Finally, because so much of what we buy is highly specific, we inevitably end up needing more; this applies to everything from kitchenware to exercise equipment to garden tools and consumer electronics. Small wonder that the American Builders Association reports that the single most desirable feature in a new house these days is a plethora of enormous closets!

• • •

Several patterns emerge as we consider the various ways in which our domestic lives have grown more demanding.

First, we see that the choices that confront us—about how we manage our money and our health, raise our children, select our cars, make our travel plans, purchase basic goods—have become so loaded with options that wading through them requires an incredible amount of concentration, time, and skill. Consumer product and services companies recognize the problem. A study commissioned by Procter & Gamble revealed that *the* major hurdle new products now face in gaining acceptance is that people are overwhelmed by excessive choice. Nevertheless, companies seem powerless to stop the endless proliferation. They fear that if they miss out on a single product variation—triple chocolate chip ice cream with macadamia nuts *and* almonds, mustard with bourbon *and* honey, peppermint-flavored floss, speed dial to reach fifty people, fleece gloves with steering wheel grips—they will leave an unexploited niche that a savvy competitor will rush to fill.

Most of us anticipate that things will become easier as we select an ever-larger proportion of our goods and services over the Internet, since part of the problem today is that we are using industrial-era delivery systems (such as big stores) to distribute a postindustrial array of services and products. However, as anyone who has repeatedly had to return items ordered via catalog knows all too well, new methods of procurement present frustrations of their own, requiring us to time our deliveries carefully and to punch in tracking codes on UPS phone trees, thus adding more items to our already crowded list of to-dos and more paperwork to keep track of. In addition, the Internet makes *everything in the world* available to us (at least in theory), a daunting prospect that requires us to become more savvy and to do more research to determine precisely what it is we really want.

Second, it becomes apparent that the speed of technology cycles creates new needs even as it satisfies them. If we buy a digital camera, we create a need for new ways of developing and displaying the photos we take. If we buy a digitized audio-tape Walkman, we create a need to buy new tapes. And as the price of new technologies plummets, it makes less sense *not* to get the new products, especially when our old products begin to fail and we compare the cost of repair with replacement. In this way, what were formerly considered luxuries have been re-defined as needs. How can a color television be a luxury when 93 percent of people in the United States living *below* the poverty line own at least one? As Kevin Kelly, editor at large for *Wired* magazine, notes, "Each actualization of desire cre-ates a platform for new technologies to create and supply new needs."

In other words, *it's endless,* this constant upping of the ante. And it threatens to trap us in an ever-escalating web of de-cisions about what to buy, where, how, from whom, why, what upgrades to get, when to switch. As with the technologies we use at work, the process is *programmed* to exhaust us by virtue of its speed, its intricacy, and its capacity for change.

Whether we choose to regard this situation as wasteful and purposeless, or view it as positive, a proof of vitality and source of job creation, doesn't matter. It's *here,* and it's not go-ing to change. The challenge for each of us is to make satisfying choices and learn to savor what we have rather than simply leaping onto a ceaseless treadmill of endless optimizing.

The third pattern that emerges as we examine the reasons our private lives have become so complex is that large numbers of us are living in ways *that only rich people used to live.* Stock portfolios, financial advisers, tennis instructors (for adults and kids), wine tastings, lawn services, different cars for various uses, not to mention five-thousand-square-foot houses: such things used to be indicators of serious wealth. What has happened over the last twenty years is a democratization of what used to be the prerogatives of upper-class life. Few of us, however, have the support systems that used to enable the wealthy to lead complex financial lives, maintain multiple vehicles, and offer children highly specialized activities—the servants, retainers, and professional managers that made their lives go smoothly. We, by contrast, have only ourselves to manage all the work that our daily lives increasingly require.

Finally, our lives are more complex simply because we *know* more, have more potential sources of information, and so are inclined to take an activist approach to our problems. If we contract a major illness, for example, we are likely to read books about it, visit medical websites, explore alternative treatments, and join support groups for people who share our experience. In short, we are more likely to become self-taught experts on our problems and to collaborate with the professionals who serve and treat us, instead of simply following their advice.

Similarly, if one of our children has trouble learning to read or seems unable to acquire a routine skill, we seek professional guidance, contact other parents whose children face similar challenges, and perhaps band together with them to create an advocacy group to explore new care options. Parental activism, neighborhood activism, environmental activism, patient activism, single-issue activism ranging from Mothers Against Drunk Driving to grassroots efforts aimed at influencing what textbooks are chosen by the local school board: *all* these have become commonplace over the last thirty years. This phenomenon gives us far greater power and control over our individual destinies, and creates more textured and satisfying ways of being in the world. But it also contributes to the professionalizing of our lives and our leisure.

Because our private lives have become more demanding at the same time that our work lives have, we may find it difficult to enjoy—or even recognize—the benefits of life in our era. Yet they are many: a lessened dependence upon large organizations, greater flexibility in how we live and work, easy access to information that was formerly restricted, the crumbling of oppressive hierarchies of control, an end to generic ways of living that gave little scope for personal choice.

However, the very freedom we have to make so many choices now lies at the heart of our common dilemma. This brings to mind the old adage about being careful what you wish for. For *choice*—economic, political, social, familial, recreational, reproductive—is the pivot upon which the last few hundred years of history have turned. People have sought choice in every arena. They have campaigned for it, demanded it, fought for it, died for it. They did their job well, with the extraordinary result that choice itself has now become our problem.

It may not *feel* as if choice is our problem. We may indeed feel as if we're locked into patterns that now lie beyond our control. But this is usually the result of previous decisions we have made in response to the plethora of choices that we faced: about work, about how we run our households, about our daily schedule.

The only way out is to become more conscious about *all* our choices, to be absolutely clear about what we need and what we do not, what serves our true purpose and what is superfluous. We must find ways to pursue elegance and simplicity in all our decisions, aligning them with what lies deepest within us, and adapting them as our needs and interests evolve. We must seek out ways of living and working that allow for greater flow and wholeness, enabling us to take advantage of (or when necessary, resist) what technology has wrought.

In the chapters ahead, we will explore ways to do this.

PART TWO

Six Strategies for Thriving in 24/7

A wonderful harmony is created when we join to-gether the seemingly unconnected.

Heraclitus, *Fragments*

3

Strategy One:
Start at the Core

When I began the interviews that became this book, I assumed that the first strategy for thriving in 24/7 would be creating your own work, even if you stayed in your job (see Strategy Three, Chapter 5). But the more people I spoke with, the more I came to recognize that this is rarely the first step. Almost everyone had gone through a period of searching before finding the work he or she really wanted to do. Most had made at least one false start; some had made many. Quite a few had begun careers they had then abandoned because the work proved uncongenial, or because the field they entered changed beyond recognition.

Listening to their stories, I began to realize that, if we want to create work that suits our individual needs and talents, we must not only be aware of the forces reshaping our world. We must also develop a thorough knowledge of ourselves and an understanding of what we have to offer. Only then can we set about finding the point of intersection between our opportunities and our gifts.

In other words, we have to *start at the core*.

We have to know our priorities, values, temperament, character, and ambitions. We have to understand where our blocks lie, what emotional legacies might be holding us back or pushing us forward. We have to understand what we fear, what makes us feel stuck or overwhelmed.

Starting at the core is crucial in our era because we have so many choices. New technologies and globalization are giving rise to whole new categories of work. At the same time, the trend toward meeting the needs of diverse and customized markets has begun to produce a demand for highly specific skills combined in distinct and highly individual ways. Thus, the era of generic career choice—teacher, doctor—is being supplanted by more niche-focused positions: FBI agent with a fluency in Mandarin, marketing consultant to nonprofits in the field of middle-school education, event planner serving the country-music industry.

This emphasis on the niche gives us more opportunities to create work that reflects our individual interests.

We also have more opportunities to determine how we market our skills. We can work for a big company, form a partnership, go solo, serve a single client. We can make our own choices because we are less dependent upon organizations than people in the past. Until the last decade or so, only the boldest entrepreneur would have considered going around or outside established organizations, because organizations served as intermediaries between people and the marketplace. Today, we have greater autonomy because we can connect with markets ourselves. This in turn gives us more opportunities to define the nature of our work.

And so, if you are a college teacher who believes there's an audience for your views on the medieval economy, you can offer a satellite course to students all over the globe in association with a lifelong learning center.

If you are a graphic designer who wants to work in a visually cutting-edge firm, you can become expert in a software program that enables you to target opportunities with architects.

If you are a human resources director who loves working with salespeople and wants to stand out in a crowded field, you can develop a sales training program designed for organizations undergoing mergers.

If you are a small-town sausage maker whose bratwurst has all the locals talking, you can hook up with a catalog company and sell your products to pork lovers across the land.

The key is to think in a broader but also more focused way.

Starting at the core is also crucial because the 24/7 workplace has become so demanding. Our work today consumes more of our time. It also consumes more of our energy because, in an economy based upon knowledge, just showing up is not enough. We need to bring our minds and spirits to work. We must be fully present, deeply engaged. Since we have to give so much of ourselves, we want work that meets our needs and offers fulfillment.

Russ Moxley, an author and executive coach at the Center for Creative Leadership in Greensboro, North Carolina, has witnessed a growing thirst among clients for work that has meaning. He says, "I hear it all the time now. People say, 'If I'm going to give *this* much of myself on the job, I want work that is meaningful and lets me express who I am. I can't motivate myself to work this hard for just a paycheck!'" Moxley also believes that people increasingly want a "rich, integrated experience of life. And you can't really have that if your work doesn't meet the needs of your spirit."

Judith Gerberg, a New York City career consultant who has been counseling people for twenty-five years, agrees with Moxley. She observes, "It used to be common for me to see people who had just sort of fallen into their work. They hadn't really given much thought to what they wanted to do. But because their work wasn't all that demanding, they didn't start to question their choices until they hit midlife. *Then* they started wondering about issues of purpose and meaning. Today, all that's changed. I see people just out of college or business school who get what they think is a terrific job. Then within a year or two, they realize they're being worked to death. So they start examining everything: their values, their goals, what's important to them as individuals, what they really want to be doing with their lives."

Gerberg notes that what she's describing used to be called a "midlife crisis." "But you can't call it that now, because it's happening with people at every age. Plus it's not a crisis anymore. It's more like a necessary *stage* that people have to go through. It's a turning point, the time when you look inward and ask the big questions, such as *who am I* and *how do I want to spend my days?* Once you've asked those questions, you can't be content with an unsatisfying job. You have to search for a way of working that's in sync with who you *are.*"

The richness and intensity of the world in which we find ourselves offers plenty of scope for self-invention. More and more, *we* get to decide how our lives will play out. In the past, people tended to follow whatever path seemed appropriate, given their family, education, connections, social class, and gender. And so the difficult work of self-discovery and self-examination—of "composing a life," to use anthropologist Mary Catherine Bateson's useful phrase—was left to the great leader, the exceptional individual.

No more. Today, we all have the chance to compose our own lives. It's a liberating prospect, but also daunting, because it requires a high degree of self-knowledge. If we *don't* start at the core—if we instead accept reflexive, inherited, or half-thought-out definitions of who we are and what we have to contribute—we run the risk of being overwhelmed by the possibilities that we face. We will then either make inappropriate choices that hinder us from fully using our individual talents and so hold us back from achieving fulfillment, or we will become what journalist David Brooks aptly calls "bobos in paradise," people who achieve the appearance of success, yet end up pursuing dreams they never bothered to think through.

But how exactly are we supposed to go about cultivating this clear sense of ourselves? How do we make time for the introspection required to come to terms with our essential natures, when our days with their heavy demands are moving by at warp speed? How do we get a sense of our own uniqueness and form an understanding of how to manifest it when the possibilities for doing so seem endless?

As is generally true in today's niche-oriented, highly customized culture, *there is no one-size-fits-all single best way to go about the task of identifying what work is best for us.* There are instead many ways to better understand precisely what we might do. These include:

❖ Confronting your personal history
❖ Locating your inner voice
❖ Getting comfortable in the neutral zone
❖ Taking inventory on a regular basis

Confronting your personal history

To know who you are and discover what you want, you have to start with where you came from. You have to perceive what shaped you and who helped make you what you are.

The people I interviewed who were most innovative in creating work that met their needs stressed the importance of doing this. They understood that an environment that encourages and rewards continual self-invention also requires that we connect with our deepest roots. And they recognized that living in a world characterized by volatility, uncertainty, complexity, and ambiguity makes it particularly important that we identify the most profound sources of our own stability, certainty, simplicity, and clarity.

An example is Carlos Marin, a coach who works with international executives. Carlos is based in San Diego, but his work takes him to Brazil, Mexico, and Spain as well as all over the United States. He is a soft-voiced and introspective man in his early fifties who passionately believes that anyone seeking to operate in our 24/7 world must start with a clear understanding of his or her character and values.

"People and organizations are incredibly diverse these days, and changing all the time," says Carlos. "That makes it more important than ever that you come from a place of being really *authentic.* You won't have the breadth, the humanity, the empathy, or the capacity to make yourself understood by a wide range of people from different cultures and backgrounds unless you have a strong understanding of yourself. Your groundedness, your center. *That's* the point from which you need to communicate. And I don't believe you can do this in an effective way unless you have a sense of connection with your own past. That's hard to do now, since we all move around so much. But that makes it even more important."

Carlos's most powerful tool for connecting with his past is learning more about his own history and that of his family. He says, "I have become very aggressive about pursuing this, about finding ways to connect with what's long-lasting. For example, whenever I go back to Costa Rica, where I grew up, I try to spend as much time as possible interviewing people who have been a part of my past. It's a process of discovery, and it connects me with what's long-lasting and important. I think this is absolutely necessary, especially if, like me, you're always traveling and have gone through a lot of personal changes. You need to put yourself more in touch with what *hasn't* changed."

Carlos points out that, when interviewing people who have played a part in your history, "It doesn't matter if someone seems strange or irrelevant. An old uncle who's been outside the family circle for years might have an important insight about your parents or your hometown that helps put everything else in perspective. So you need to spend time with him, and with other such people. Not just in aimless conversation, but very deliberately. You should try to get them to tell their stories, ask them questions. And you should write down or tape what they have to say. The more you learn about all the things that shaped you, the more clues you uncover, and the more you will understand who you have become."

In addition to family members, Carlos tries to interview people he grew up with, engaging them in far-reaching conversation about what influenced the course of their lives. "There's a group of men I know from my high school days, and we get together whenever I'm in my country. We used to just go to a bar and talk about fairly superficial topics. But then, because I had been interviewing people in my family, I began trying to shift the tone of our conversations."

Carlos started asking them what they remembered that shaped their lives, what they recalled about him and about one another. "I wanted to learn what was impactful that had happened when we were kids, so I could get a sense of what had shaped me. I really learned a lot. For example, one of my high school friends reminded me how much I used to enjoy listening to shortwave radio programs from other countries, how intrigued I was by the exotic-sounding languages. That made me remember how closely I used to listen to sounds and intonations, how I loved imitating different kinds of speech and fantasizing that I could communicate in different languages. Various relatives confirmed the story and added dimensions to it. One cousin described how I would respond in 'Arabic' or 'Chinese' to my mother's request that I pass the butter. I also developed the ability to mimic different Spanish accents. This was a big part of my childhood that I had forgotten."

Carlos became aware of how this childhood curiosity had shaped his life, beginning with his formal study of various foreign languages. He says, "Today I travel all around the world helping executives develop their leadership and communication skills. This requires me to empathize and understand the kinds of issues my clients deal with and to be very attentive to their speech. My ability to pick up intonations, my sensitivity to that, is an important skill. And it's a grown-up version of what I used to do as a kid."

When Carlos began coaxing his friends to share their memories, they weren't comfortable doing so at first. "I had to work on it, I had to persevere. But gradually, they became interested in what I was doing. Now we share some profound memories with one another, and of course this has brought us much closer."

Carlos suggests using a similar kind of guided conversation at high school or college reunions as well as when visiting family. "Once you establish that you are interested in other people's specific memories of your common past, you will get a reputation for that. And then they will begin seeking you out so they can tell you what they remember. This enables you to discover the role these people played in your own life, as well as the role you might have played in theirs. All these inquiries help you to understand how your roots have shaped your destiny."

Stanley Siegel, a psychotherapist in private practice in New York, agrees that confronting one's personal history is essential in today's environment. But he stresses the role that self-invention plays in spurring individuals to look closely at their own pasts.

He says, "Until recently, the opportunity for self-invention was not an option for most people. Society placed great value on tradition, so self-invention was considered the province of the artist or the renegade. It was usually perceived as being *dangerous.* Now, people are rewarded and celebrated for it. Self-invention has become part of the capitalist and consumer framework. At the same time, there's more of a dialogue in the general culture about questions of meaning and purpose. It has become *okay,* acceptable, to delve into your personal past. We are exposed to people doing it in the media. Sure, the way it's handled on some of the talk shows can be pretty tasteless. But on the whole, it creates a more inquisitive attitude that helps people sort out who they are and what they really want to be."

In such an environment, Siegel observes, it is particularly important that we look closely at our family of origin. "You need to try to discern the messages you got from your family. Especially the messages regarding work and money, entitlement and ambition. Those messages might be at variance with the opportunities you face, or with what you really want from your life. Or they might reflect a system of values you've outgrown." Even so, such messages can hold you back if you don't find a way to work through them consciously, either in therapy or with a personal coach.

Siegel points to the example of a musician he treated. "He had the talent to go to the absolute top as a concert player, and that's what he really wanted. He knew he had the potential, so he felt he was a failure because he hadn't made it happen. He came from a poor but close-knit, loving family that had a picture of itself as being very happy. It *was* happy, but it was also very invested in this picture. So the message he got was, *It's not important to have material success or fame or to love your work. Your family is enough. We're not rich or ambitious, but we've always been happy.* Because this was his family's message, his becoming highly successful would have been seen as divisive. It would have indicated that his family *wasn't* enough for him, that he wanted more. So he kept his sights low and found ways to sabotage himself out of a sense of loyalty to his family. But it made him miserable because he really wanted that musical career."

Other patients Siegel works with have the opposite problem. In their families, success is highly desirable and even expected, but is defined entirely by money. "People from such families," he notes, "often leave their real talents unexplored because they fear that doing so would cost them financially. For them, *not* focusing on money would be the ultimate betrayal, evidence that they are disloyal to their family's values."

Siegel's description reminded me of a successful publishing executive I know who has become frustrated since his magazine was bought by a conglomerate known for its arbitrary and authoritarian management style. As a result of how he is treated, this man no longer feels respected on the job and is unable to have much impact upon his publication. However, he has a brilliant reputation and has been approached by investors eager to back him in a new venture. The idea thrills him, but he hasn't been able to make the leap.

He says, "What holds me back is the money. I've come to *hate* what I'm doing, but I can't risk leaving. I'd have to take a substantial salary cut, which would impact my family's standard of living, which is fairly luxurious but it's what we've gotten used to. And of course, there's always the possibility that something new might fail." This man admits that his powerful father's message to him was, *A man's only as good as his checkbook. You're a fool if you work for anything but money.*

"I don't subscribe to that view," he insists, pointing out that he entered publishing against his father's wishes. Nevertheless, his financial success has served as proof of his loyalty to his father's code. And he now finds himself wretched at work but absolutely stuck despite considerable success, because he has not been able to free himself of his family's values. As with the musician Stanley Siegel treated, this talented man won't be able to carve out a satisfying path for himself until he begins to come to terms with his father's legacy and understands the impact it has had upon him.

Our ability to reinvent ourselves (and the need to confront our history that this creates) is a major reason that therapy has become so popular over the last two decades. Yet a number of people I spoke with had, like Carlos Marin, found less traditional ways of connecting with their pasts. Several had made extraordinary life changes as a result.

Erin Thomas is one of them. When I first met Erin several years ago, she was a successful marketing entrepreneur who had worked in advertising, then started her own company north of San Diego. Tall, outgoing, and confident in her late thirties, Erin had a wide network of friends and seemed happy in her work. Two years later, when I met her again, I was surprised to find her studying for the ministry, living close to the bone to support the cost of graduate school. When I asked her about this surprising career shift, she explained that it resulted from a period of intense searching during which she spent considerable time exploring her past.

Erin says, "I always liked my work, and I was good at it. Then all of a sudden, when I hit my mid-thirties, I began to have this feeling that something was missing." Echoing what Judith Gerberg observed about premature midlife crises, Erin adds, "I think my dissatisfaction was pretty typical for someone my age who hadn't given enough thought to what I really wanted to do. When I look at my parents, I see that everything was kind of determined for them in advance. They did what was expected, given their age and their gender. For my generation, things are different. There's this huge menu of stuff that we can do. It's great, but it also makes life harder. We're free to live as we want, and we see people around us doing these incredible things. So we're more likely to become discontented if we start to feel we're not reaching our potential."

Erin reacted to her dissatisfaction by going "on a kind of quest. I became obsessed with the idea of trying to find my true purpose in life: why I was here, how I was meant to use my talents." At first, she worked with a career coach, hoping this might lead to some answers. Together they did Meyers Briggs (the personality assessment tool used by many organizations) and all the standard aptitude tests. But Erin didn't feel that the work went deep enough.

Because her confusion seemed rooted in an inner emptiness that she was becoming aware of, Erin talked about it with the spiritual director at the large Presbyterian church she had recently joined. The adviser started Erin on a program. "First, I did a workshop on taking inventory of your spiritual gifts. But I also worked on confronting my past. The idea was that if I knew more about the forces that had shaped me, I could be more conscious in making my future choices."

Erin's adviser suggested she begin by creating a chart of her life history, using a timeline to mark significant dates. "The timeline was like one you'd see in a history book. It started with my birth and continued up to the present. Above the line, I wrote down all my major experiences and tied them to specific years: where I was living, when I went to college, my first job, my marriage, promotions, my divorce. All the *events,* all the things I did."

Below the timeline, Erin wrote down everything she could remember about her personal development as it corresponded with each event. She worked from diaries and calendars, spending hours coaxing memories to the surface. "I tried to get a feeling for what was going on inside me at different times in my life. What preoccupied me during a given year? What was I dreaming? What did I feel conflicted about? What were my worries? What did I believe in? What did I fear? What did I feel good about? The idea was to get a sense of a story unfolding on two levels, the inner and the outer. I was working to get a clear picture not just of what happened, but also of what it *meant,* using as much detail as possible."

Creating the timeline gave Erin the confidence she needed to pursue her quest. "What I realized," she reflects, "is that I have this pattern. About every four years, I go through a major upheaval. It's always a difficult time for me, emotionally and usually financially as well. But getting through it leads to some kind of epiphany and from that comes major and positive change." Seeing her pattern manifest in visual form helped Erin recognize that the search she was on "wasn't flakey. It wasn't even especially unusual for me. *That* gave me the confidence I needed to continue with my explorations, instead of just feeling that I was spinning my wheels."

Erin's adviser also had her create a "geneagram," as a way of uncovering further patterns and details and forcing her to delve more deeply into her past. Erin explains, "Basically, a geneagram is a kind of map of your extended family, going back as many generations as you can. It's like a family tree: you use squares for males, circles for females. You fill in everything visually: lines for children, connectors for marriages, marks across lines for divorces. You show separations and relationships where people have fallen out of touch. You use Xs for abortions, squiggly lines for abusive relationships. You try to get as complete a picture as you can, the good and the bad. You tag on notes about job changes, moves, illnesses or depressions people went through."

Working on the geneagram, Erin became aware of how much she didn't know about her family. And so, she began interviewing people, as Carlos Marin had done. She recalls, "Once I really got people in my family talking, so much came out! Family secrets, disappointments my parents had lived with, ambitions and talents they never explored. Regrets, paths not taken, what drove and inspired the people in my family to do what they did and live as they chose."

Just as the timeline had revealed personal patterns, so the geneagram revealed family patterns. Erin says, "For example, I saw that in my family, the men have tended to be fairly passive and non-risktaking, while the women, even though they were mostly homemakers, were social change agents in their communities. They were feminists, really, though they never would have described themselves that way. Once I realized this, I got a strong sense that *I* could be a pathbreaker if I wanted, and do something out of the ordinary for a woman. It would be in the family tradition."

As she was learning more about her past and her family, Erin was also exploring her gifts in a workshop offered at her church. The idea behind the workshop was not just to help people explore their talents, but to then encourage them to use their gifts as volunteers in the church. "What I learned from the workshop," says Erin, "is that I have this cluster of gifts around communication. I'm good at speaking, writing, and teaching. Of course, I'd done a lot of speaking and writing in my work as a marketer, but the workshop urged me to use those talents for the benefit of my congregation. So I got more active, giving talks and readings during services, and participating in and leading retreats."

It was the feedback she got from these activities that led her to consider the ministry. "People kept saying, 'you're perfect for this.' And I felt it too." At first, Erin thought about working to become a professional speaker, and she hired a coach to develop her skills. But that experience only made her realize that she was most comfortable using her gifts in the context of the church.

"When you're really working to find your true purpose," she says, "you go through a kind of process of elimination and refinement. Sometimes what you're aiming at comes in a surprise package. That was certainly true for me! It was really the affirmation I got, along with what I learned about myself by

confronting my past, that finally gave me the clarity to understand what I was supposed to be doing."

Locating your inner voice

Ralph Waldo Emerson observed that "Every man's condition is
a solution in hieroglyphic to the inquiries that he would put. He
lives it in life before he perceives it as truth."

Most of us have known the experience of having an intima-
tion that we will do something before we are in a position to do
it, or before we are even consciously aware that we *want* to do
it. Most of us have intuited subtle hints about the direction in
which our destiny lies. These hints, these foretastes, these "hi-
eroglyphs" of which Emerson writes, come to us in the form of
an inner voice. Locating and accessing that inner voice—better
yet, being able to draw upon its wisdom at will—can give us a
clearer picture of what lies at our core, while putting us more
profoundly in touch with what our lives are becoming.

Many of the people I interviewed for this book who had
found innovative ways to match their talents to unexpected opportunities spoke openly about the extent to which they had let
their inner voice guide them. Listening to them, I began to realize that the inner voice is especially useful in a frontier period
such as ours, when new ways of working and living are rapidly
evolving, and new ideas and new kinds of organizations are being born. Because none of us can be sure how these changes
will play out in our own lives (we are told that fully 70 percent
of the work that we now do will be obsolete in twenty years),
intuitive ways of knowing assume a greater value than in eras

when life was more predictable and settled. The capacity to listen to our inner voice—to perceive our life in hieroglyph—can be a powerful means of connecting ourselves with an unfolding future that cannot be comprehended by logic alone.

I had originally sought to interview Barbara Roberts, a smart, well-connected, and accomplished executive, because I wanted her thoughts on innovative ways to build a strong and supportive network (see Strategy Four, Chapter 6). Barbara is CEO of Acoustiguide, a company that develops interactive audio programs for museums from Beijing to London to New York. Her career has been rich and turbulent, full of change and achievement. She started on Wall Street in the early 1970s and became successful quickly, landing on her firm's board of directors at an early age. When the company was bought, her new boss informed her that she would not be invited onto the executive committee because having a woman present would make the men uncomfortable.

Barbara quit—"the CEO was shocked," she says—and ended up in a special edition of the *Wall Street Journal,* identified as one of three women who had hit the "glass ceiling." Barbara went on to assume a CEO position in a media company before taking her present job, and to serve on a variety of nonprofit boards. As a result, she has a broad and varied range of friends, colleagues, contacts, and supporters. I wanted her insights into building and maintaining a strong web of support.

Barbara, however, surprised me by stressing that "while having a network is important, at the end of the day your real support system is basically yourself. And I think that's terribly important for people to understand *now,* when there are so many choices to be made, so many ways to live and work. It's easy to get overwhelmed and waste your life doing things that aren't right for you, which is what happens if you listen to too many people and get too many opinions. Because things are so wide open, you need to be very clear about your purpose in life. And the best way I've found to do that is to listen to my inner voice."

The process by which Barbara Roberts coaxes forth that voice is highly conscious and disciplined. For her, the capacity to *know oneself* isn't something we are born with, but something we develop by using specific techniques. "For example," she says, "as soon as I get up in the morning I sit down with a notebook and just start writing whatever comes to me—automatically, not thinking, not censoring, just letting it *flow.* I do this because I believe that when you're sleeping, your brain continues to work on your problems and issues. What you need and who you are becoming makes itself apparent in a way that is not intellectual, but is nevertheless very real. So by writing down whatever comes to you first thing in the morning, you are in essence *downloading* your deepest thoughts, making them accessible, part of your conscious memory bank. And this gives you a way to tap into a kind of inner wisdom that is easy to lose touch with during the course of the day because you get so buried in the details of living."

Barbara knows this process works because she has kept the notebooks in which she has written for many years. She says, "It's almost eerie to see how what I write in my journals shows up in my life after a few years, though not always in the way I would have expected. For example, when I was on Wall Street, my journals reflected a strong desire to do something more creative and to be involved with people in the arts. Later, when I was looking for a CEO position, I was offered the chance to lead a photography company that brought me into contact with just the kind of people I had wanted to be around." Reading her earlier journals thus confirmed Barbara's intuition that this position was the right one for her. "Later, after I'd sold the company, I had lots of opportunities to lead technology companies. But my journals showed that I still wanted to be involved in the arts and that I was yearning to do a lot of international travel." And so when the Acoustiguide opportunity presented itself, Barbara took it.

Reading back over her journal entries has enabled Barbara to understand "why I'm here and what I'm trying to accomplish. And because I understand that, what I need sort of falls into place. I'm a big believer in the idea of resting in my karma—identifying it, accepting it, moving toward it. By karma, I don't mean a predetermined fate. I mean the destiny that I have *chosen* to embrace. My inner voice is my point of connection with my karma. Because I do my writing in the morning, I'm in touch with the destiny that I am moving toward."

Barbara draws upon her inner voice when she needs to make decisions. "I use a three part system," she explains. "First, I ask myself what happened in the past, both good and bad, that might be affecting my judgment or influencing how I am inclined. Then I ask myself what is the best thing and the worst thing that could happen if I make this decision. Finally, I divide myself up into three parts—my head, my heart, and my gut. I write down what each of those parts wants to do. For my head, I put down all the rational arguments. For my heart, I look at the decision in terms of what I feel most passionate about just now. For my gut, I put down my physical reactions, how it makes me feel. The goal is to bring every thought and every fear into consciousness, so I will have as much information as possible."

Barbara believes this technique can be helpful in avoiding the kind of generic decisions people so often make that don't reflect their individual needs. She says, "I see it all the time, people making these very logical and predetermined lists of what they think they want out of life. A woman, for example, will say, 'By the time I'm 35, I want to have a husband and two kids. I want to be senior VP of a company and be making *x* amount of dollars.' When I hear someone talking like that, I always wonder if she's thought through *why* she wants a husband, *why* she wants those kids, *why* she thinks *x* amount of money will satisfy her. What if she meets the wrong guy? Will she marry him anyway, just to meet some self-imposed deadline? Will she hold onto a job she hates because it enables her to make that specific amount of money? It sounds ridiculous, put that way, but it happens all the time. And I think one reason it does is that people don't have a good system for making decisions, a system that really takes advantage of their inner voice."

Karen Van Dyke, an extremely warm and outgoing woman in her mid-forties, is a former event marketer from southern California who recently moved to Orlando, where her husband had accepted a job with Disney. In Florida, she has reinvented herself as a marketing consultant for online ventures, and immediately helped organize a regional Internet conference.

Karen has a very deliberate approach to accessing her inner voice. Like Barbara Roberts, she records her dreams in a journal each morning. She rereads her notebooks to get a sense of the patterns that thread through her life and to identify the foreshadowings of events that later prove important. However, she adds the particular twist of giving herself what she calls "dream assignments" as a means of inviting her inner voice—or what Karen calls her *knowingness*—to tell her what she needs to understand.

Karen says, "When I have something important I need to work through, I take time alone before I go to bed to think about what I need in terms of guidance. I then write out a couple of specific questions, and read them over to myself several times out loud. After that, I literally *ask* for a dream that will give me the answer to my dilemma or point out the course of action I should take. As I fall asleep, I try to concentrate on what I have asked. I keep a notebook by my bed so I can jot down what I'm dreaming if I wake up during the night. Then in the morning, I write down everything I can remember."

Karen says the messages she gets from her dreams are often veiled, and take a few days or even weeks to figure out. At other times, the message is absolutely clear. For example, last year she was trying to decide whether to follow her husband to Florida or stay in California, which she loved and where she felt at home. She hated the thought of moving, but feared her marriage would suffer if she did not. Feeling tormented and unable to choose, she asked for a dream that would give her the answer.

That night, she had a vivid dream about being in the *Wizard of Oz.* "And the wicked witch kept saying very clearly, 'Surrender, Dorothy!' Only *I* was Dorothy in the dream, and she was telling *me* to surrender. I interpreted that to mean I should just give in, and trust that everything would be all right. So I did. I packed up and moved to Orlando. It's been a hard adjustment, but I haven't questioned or regretted it, because I feel strongly that it's what I'm *supposed* to be doing. If I hadn't had that dream, I wouldn't feel such confidence. I would probably still be torn. And in my experience, it's having confidence that makes things happen. And I need all the confidence I can get to make things work out here."

As Barbara and Karen demonstrate, the inner voice can be a guide to making decisions or a means of becoming comfortable with an intuitive response. But it can also take the form of an insistent and underlying discontent with your circumstances that pushes you to make needed change. Psychotherapist Stanley Siegel describes the inner voice as "the voice of *longing.*" He says, "It's about longings that have gone unfulfilled. It's an expression of unrequited desires. It makes you aware of desires that you want to act on but might be afraid of, because you've made a conscious and rational decision that you *should* do something else." Locating the inner voice, as Siegel defines it, is a way of bringing unexpressed desires to light, so you can mesh the core of your being with how you are living your daily life.

This notion of the inner voice as a voice of longing was experienced by Chad Alcorn of Chicago. Chad, now thirty-two, landed a promising job right out of college, placing advertising for a group of medical magazines. He says, "I hadn't given all that much thought to what I wanted to do in life. I'd been a football player all through high school and had a football scholarship in college, so my whole self-concept was based on being an athlete. Going into the business world seemed like a natural thing, and that's what all my friends were doing. I was basically motivated by the idea of *being* a success, but had no idea of what that meant to me. Right away, I started making good money, and for the first couple of years, I enjoyed it. I liked buying things, saving money and having freedom."

But when Chad was twenty-six, he entered a period of crisis. "It started because I felt dissatisfied with all the traveling and the constant pressure. The industry was consolidating, and that made for a huge load of work. Things began to seem very unbalanced. I'd wake up in some hotel and wonder where I was, what city. I started to feel as if I had no control over my life. So I began asking myself, *what if I keep doing this?* I'll make more money, but what will that mean? That I'll play more golf, take more vacations, buy a bigger house? I began to see that I was someone who needed more out of life than just being motivated by money. It was right around this time that I remember looking at some medical magazine and thinking that I didn't see how a certain ad placement would make any difference for the product. Well, you can't be great at sales with *that* kind of attitude! You've got to believe in what you're doing. I took that as a sign that it was time for me to get out."

Chad's recognition that his work had lost meaning for him sent him into what he calls "my existential period." "I remember listening to a song called *The Amazing Journey,*" he recalls.

"I would play it over and over and think, *that's what my life could be.*" In Stanley Siegel's terms, he had begun to listen to the voice of longing.

Around this time, Chad began to make regular visits to his parents, who live in a Chicago suburb, where his father is a psychologist and his mother an academic dean. "I was looking at my past, thinking a lot about my family of origin, how it had influenced me. I realized that I'd gotten away from some of the values I shared with my parents. I remember one night at a party hearing some of my dad's clients talking about what an impact he'd had on their lives. And I thought, *that's what life's really about.*"

And so, at the age of twenty-eight, Chad entered a Ph.D. program in clinical psychology. He is writing his dissertation on how career stress affects families. "Now my sales and marketing experience seems like an advantage, instead of something that has nothing to do with me. It gives me something to offer, makes me feel I can create a real niche for myself. I can develop programs that bring organizational and family psychology together, two fields that have been treated like separate universes." Despite the sacrifices he's made—"I'm thirty-two and an impoverished graduate student, living with a roommate and working harder than I've ever worked in my life"—Chad takes pride and satisfaction in having heeded the voice of his own discontent.

Getting comfortable in the neutral zone

I first heard the term "the neutral zone" from Bill Bridges, a consultant and author in Mill Valley, California, who helps individuals and companies deal with transition. Bill speaks of "going to the neutral zone" to describe what we experience when we are moving out of an old way of life but are not psychologically ready for the new life that we will be living. It's a condition many of us face when struggling to reinvent our lives.

Bill adapted the notion of the neutral zone from an early-twentieth-century anthropologist, Arnold Van Gennep, who wrote about the crucial role that rites of passage play in tribal societies. Van Gennep found that, in such cultures, distinctive rituals help people through times of transition, which are considered important emotional landmarks in human life. While undergoing periods of transition, people spend time alone in the desert, walk a dangerous path for many miles, retire to an isolated hut in the woods, adopt a totem animal, or work on a difficult project under the tutelage of an elder.

These demanding and rigorous activities, which lie outside the realm of the everyday, prepare people to enter a new stage in their lives. Western culture, of course, doesn't offer any rituals or practices to help us through such periods. We tend to speak of being in transition as "being in limbo," which has no positive or dynamic connotations at all. In Western theology, limbo is one step up from hell.

Bill Bridges points out that entry into the neutral zone often follows some kind of trauma, such as losing a job, realizing that the career we have chosen is not for us, or confronting major illness or divorce. Such events throw us back upon ourselves and make us question our decisions. "Being in the neutral zone," says Bridges, "is really about asking, *quo vadis?* That is, *where am I going?* What am I getting ready to do? In what direction should I be headed? How can I best use my gifts in the years ahead?"

To make room for the answers to these questions to emerge, we have to draw back from our daily lives. That's what Chad Alcorn did when he went through his "existential crisis." It's what Erin did when she went on her "quest." Psychotherapist Stanley Siegel notes that during such periods, "the single most important thing you can do is *not* bury yourself in routine, because routine deadens your awareness and makes you feel secure. When you're preparing for a big change, *you need to feel a certain amount of confusion and insecurity.* So you don't want the usual crutches of daily life to prop you up. And you need to *stay* with your confusion, not try to get over it or keep it at bay. You have to hold on, wait, and be still." Meditation can be a great aid in such times, Siegel notes, because the meditative state enables answers to surface from your unconscious. At the same time, meditation is a gesture of surrender.

The neutral zone can be a fearsome place because it often feels as if *nothing* is happening, as if you are just spinning your wheels or giving way to paralysis. You don't yet have a mental image of what the rest of your life is going to be like; you are simply *waiting* for the answers you need, trusting that they will somehow come. In addition, this state of waiting can involve letting go of long-established aspects of who you are. This in itself can be profoundly unsettling.

Peggy Cappy, a medical hypnotherapist from Peterborough, New Hampshire, spent nearly a year in the neutral zone when her mother's cancer reached an advanced stage. Peggy decided to stop taking clients and teaching classes. She began spending weeks at a time at her mother's house in Houston, where she had grown up.

She says, "So much of my identity has always been in my work, in this network of clients and students that I've developed. That's *who I've been* for quite a while. But this year, I've been letting go of it. I've also been letting go of my schedule, the way I have always structured my days. When I'm with my mother, I adapt to her hours. I go to bed very early, and take naps during the day. It all feels very unsettling and purposeless, but I'm trying to have faith in the process. I'm aware that I'm taking the time to look at all the strands of who I am. And I know that, when this year is over, I will weave those strands together in a different way."

Because being in the neutral zone is disturbing, we are often tempted to just do something—*anything*—to relieve our discomfort. This is always a mistake, according to Bill Bridges. "Discomfort is *part* of it," he insists. "It is an inescapable aspect. Remember, in tribal cultures, the tasks people undertake during this time are always hard. They require endurance. Making it through the experience is what gives you the strength and skills you need to undergo a profound transition." Given that we are likely to experience more frequent (and more wrenching) transitions than people who lived in more settled eras, understanding the role of the neutral zone has particular value for us.

Getting comfortable in the neutral zone is also important because it helps us develop the kind of intuitive powers that enable us to be sensitive to our inner voice. In this regard, it is helpful to recall that the concept of the neutral zone came from studying the practices of traditional cultures. People in such cultures, finding themselves alone in a world they did not understand, had to develop ways to discern the mind of whatever god they worshiped, as well as the workings of nature. To this end, they evolved rituals that sharpened their intuition.

By contrast, Western culture has tended to view the universe as governed by predictable laws that can be discerned and described using reason and logic alone. In recent decades, however, this has begun to change. Newtonian or mechanical physics has given way to quantum and chaos theory, which share many underlying presumptions with traditional and non-Western schools of thought. Biologists too have begun to take a more holistic view, seeing all phenomena as elements in living systems that can be affected by unpredictable and seemingly unrelated events.

And so we are coming to understand the universe not as a precisely calibrated great machine in which each constituent part is locked into its own immutable slot, but rather *as pulses of energy that continually evolve and shift as the various elements interact.* By extension, we are beginning to accept the notion that we ourselves are constantly evolving, always in the process of becoming something new in response to our own innovations or changes in our environment. This is the true root of the emphasis we have begun to place on self-invention.

Our more integrated way of viewing the world has enabled us to develop more integrated and responsive technologies, which in turn are reshaping how we live and think. And because these technologies embody principles of unpredictability and relationship, using them requires us to nurture and develop a more intuitive approach.

Judith Bardwick, a La Jolla–based psychologist who studies how organizations work, describes why this is so. She says, "Almost every one of us in the Western world has been overtrained in logic. It's our heritage, part of who we are. But we can't operate just by logic in a networked economy because *it's all about networks,* and networks function like the brain. That is, they fire very quickly, and take a lot of unpredictable and sudden shortcuts. In the brain, any reaction in any synapse can set off a chain of reactions in other synapses that moves through the whole system and alters reality in a matter of seconds. Linked websites work like synapses. This is why the Internet is basically a chaotic environment in which things can change completely very fast. Logic just isn't powerful enough to deal with this. It's too literal, too linear, and *way* too slow! The upshot of all this is that we have to rely more on our gut than on time-tested logic. And so we have to figure out ways of getting more in touch with whatever our gut is telling us to do."

The world Judith Bardwick describes is, of course, the world of VUCA. It is also a world in which intuitive ways of knowing have a vital role to play. In such a world, we all need to develop a greater tolerance for the discomfort that comes of "being in limbo," recognizing and trusting that such periods of disorder, lethargy, and even apparent depression can be a valuable means of accessing exactly what we need to know.

Taking inventory on a regular basis

Starting at the core means distinguishing what is unchanging about ourselves in terms of values, character, temperament, and ambitions. But while our values may remain constant, our circumstances and desires continue to evolve, requiring us to keep in constant touch with ourselves. The best way to do this is to take our own inventory on a regular basis. The people I interviewed used a variety of means to do this. The simplest and most effective included the yearly self-audit and the daily assessment.

Chris Cappy, the president of Pilot Consultants, which is based in New Hampshire, uses the discipline of a yearly self-audit to keep on top of the changes that characterize his personal and professional life. He observes that anyone who owns a business audits profits, losses, and expenditures at the end of every year. Why not use a similar process to track how we use our energy and time?

Chris says, "The process is simple, but incredibly helpful. Every year, around January first, I take an entire day off. I sit down with my calendar for the previous year and review how I've spent my time over the past twelve months. I ask myself what I enjoyed doing, and what I did not. Then I take a sheet of paper and divide it in half. On one side I write *Things I like and want to spend more time doing.* On the other I write *Things I don't like and want to spend less time doing.*"

Having created this chart, Chris begins jotting down everything he wants more of in his life. He also makes note of "all the unsatisfying stuff I want to try to phase out. I don't think about either of these categories too much, I just let the answers

come intuitively." Nor does Chris try to differentiate between
what seems important or trivial. He then uses this information
to create a vision of what his calendar would look like if he
were to use his time in more rewarding ways. How would his
days be structured? What would their shape be like? He thinks
through the precise steps and changes in attitude that would enable him to make needed changes.

"For example," he says, "one thing I put down on the list is
that I spend too much time traveling, and want to do less of it in
the year ahead. Well, that's fine, but what are the specific ways
I could limit being on the road? Should I make more use of
technology instead of jumping on a plane every time I want to
talk to my clients? Or should I search harder for projects that
relate to my community? Should I make a rule, absolutely no
travel on weekends, ever? Would that be enough to make me
feel more in control? And what would be the impact on my income if I stayed home more? Could I live with that? Or am I
unwilling at this time to make the trade-off? Do I have financial
goals that are more important just now than my desire to cut
back on travel?"

Once Chris has thought things through concretely, he
writes down what he realistically believes he can commit to in
order to spend more time doing the things he enjoys. "I used to
put this list at the end of my calendar for the coming year," he
says. "But then I thought, *why put it at the end?* Shouldn't I use
it as my *starting* point? So now I copy out my vision for how I
want to spend my time and throw it up on the main screen of
my computer. Every time I boot up, I'm reminded of what I am
committed to, and why. I admit, the process isn't magic, but
sometimes it seems to work that way. Focused attention brings

new energy to every aspect of your life. And that's what the self-audit is really about: focusing your attention on how you want to be spending your hours and your days."

Chris finds it useful to review previous self-audits at the same time that he analyzes how he spent his time the previous year. "It's incredible," he says, "how you start to see patterns. It really teaches you about yourself. In some ways, it gives you a clear indication that you are making progress, because you see you have actually made changes over the years. But you also notice how some of the same things keep cropping up—things you *claim* you want to do, but never manage to act on. So you have to ask yourself, why not? Are those things really not so important to you? Is it just stuff you *think* you should be doing but don't actually want to do? What's blocking you, what's standing in your way? Maybe it's time to let go of something you imagine you want but never get around to pursuing. Or maybe you need a completely new plan for working it into your life."

Chris calls this reviewing of previous self-audits "the calendar test." He says it helps him to understand the extent to which his actions reveal his real values. "It's one thing to write down a list of your values," he points out. "That's something people, like organizations, are being encouraged to do these days. But you get a lot better sense of what your values actually *are* when you look at how you spend your time. Doing the calendar test provides a kind of reality check."

The calendar test enables Chris to gauge his values in a way that has had a fundamental impact on his life. He says, "We usually judge ourselves by our intentions, while others judge us by our actions. The calendar test enables you to bridge this gap, because it forces you to recognize that what you give your time to is what you really value. This was helpful to me when I went through a kind of midlife crisis at the age of forty. Doing my self-assessment that year, I could not escape the fact that I was giving a lot of time to work but no time to social action. In other words, it was pretty apparent that I was not living what I liked to think of as my values."

Chris was in a quandary about this discrepancy when a woman who worked down the hall happened to drop by his office. "It was literally a case of opportunity walking through the door. She worked for a local hospice located in our building. I knew her slightly, and she'd just stopped by to chat. But because I was thinking about my need to be more socially involved, I ended up volunteering to work at the hospice. Well, I got very involved, and became president of the board, which gave me a very different role in my community and changed the way I balance my life."

Just as the calendar test can help put us in touch with what is lacking in our lives, so can it also enable us to more realistically assess what we manage to achieve. Julie Johnson, an executive coach based in Connecticut, works with senior executives in financial services. Julie says that one of her clients' major challenges is learning how to realistically assess what they accomplish in any given day.

"The people I work with," says Julie, "are incredibly successful. But many of them feel beaten down by work. One of the ways this manifests itself is that they seem only to notice whatever it is they have *not* gotten done. They assess themselves in terms of their uncompleted tasks, which gives them an unrealistically negative picture. My role is basically to try to get them to see themselves in a more positive and optimistic light."

To this end, Julie asks clients to close out each evening by writing down three concrete things that they have accomplished during the day. "It's incredible, but often they have to struggle to do this. They'll say, 'Well, what I *didn't* do was return my marketing guy's phone call, or prepare my presentation for Monday.' I have to stress that they need to close out each day by focusing on what they *have* done, on their achievements, and let everything else go. If you can't do this, you can't realistically assess your life." Using the calendar test to gauge how you spend your time gives you a firmer grasp on your achievements.

I know the importance of accurate self-assessment, having learned it through trial and error. Several years ago, I began to feel that my own life had become hopelessly unbalanced. It was, in fact, while looking for ways to change this that I began the conversations that became this book. Like Chris Cappy, I recognized that the source of my dissatisfaction lay in how I was spending my hours and days. Yet my activities were either things I very much wanted to do, or things I did not see how I could possibly avoid without spending an unsustainable amount of money hiring people to do them for me.

My frustration came because my days felt frantic yet curiously unsatisfying. I felt as if I were living simply with the goal of checking things off my list. Because I had more tasks than I could do with ease, I was always looking to become more efficient. I had decided years before that the most efficient means of getting through the day was to devote my energies to doing one thing thoroughly.

And so I would shield myself from contact with friends so I could give all my attention to the book or article I was writing. When my writing binges left me feeling lonely, I would schedule social periods during which I would overbook myself with engagements, going from breakfasts to lunches to dinners until I felt exhausted. I would let my mail, always a potential source of distraction, pile up, then spend long and frustrating days guiltily answering correspondence and paying overdue bills. I would reserve my housekeeping and food shopping for weekends, then feel burdened that I couldn't enjoy my leisure time. I would schedule doctor-and-dentist days, time-out days at the health club. What I did not do was figure a way to integrate these activities.

One evening, I was sitting on the bus checking off my daily to-do list, which I keep in a small spiral daybook. Leafing back through the past few weeks' pages in an effort to reassure myself that I had actually gotten a few things accomplished, I was suddenly struck by what a rich and multifaceted life I actually had. The way I spent my time revealed that I took pleasure in doing different kinds of things. My core being (although I didn't think of it that way then) was characterized by a wide diversity of interests.

I also saw that I had an almost physical need to handle a lot of details and to do mundane chores. I enjoy chatting with the butcher about which cut might be best for tonight's stew. I like doing laundry in my apartment building and greeting neighbors. I even take pleasure in trips to our local copy shop, a neighborhood hangout filled with students from the college across the street. While these activities might *seem* to clutter my days, I understood that they actually give me a sense of groundedness and balance, of connectedness and belonging.

In terms of the old fable—which tells us that the hedgehog knows many things, while the fox knows one big thing—I saw clearly that I had the temperament of a hedgehog.

As I analyzed how I spent my time, my need for a diversity of experience was obvious. What *lacked* diversity, however, was the structure of my individual days. They were profoundly out of whack, devoted exhaustively to one thing or another. *This* was the reason they felt unsatisfying.

I turned to the back page of my daybook and wrote out the following list:

Friends and family
Whatever I am presently writing
Future projects
Connecting with people
Money/accounting/bills
Health and exercise
Domestic chores
Spirit and reflection
Arts, reading, entertainment

These, I decided, were all areas of importance to me. *What I needed to do was to start giving some attention to each every single day.* Therefore, my daily to-do list should include some activity related to each area, rather than focusing on a single aspect such as writing—a foxlike strategy bound to be distressing for a hedgehog. By deliberately including diverse activities, I would, in effect, be *customizing* my days to suit my particular temperament.

Because the areas to which I wanted to give attention were now listed on the last page of my daybook, I began using it in an entirely new way. Rather than composing my daily list of to-dos based upon what seemed most urgent—or what I had failed to do the previous day—I instead made sure that I scheduled at least one thing that reflected each area of interest. Instead of efficiency, I aimed for integration and balance.

A typical page under the new scheme looks like this:

JANUARY 5
Finish Chapter Three!
Mail photo for Dallas engagement
Send New Year's letters to Sandy & Charlie, Kelly & Jim
Put in for Atlanta expenses
Parmesan, ham, pine nuts, game hens
Snowshoe up Mike and Loretta's hill
Read two chapters in *A Distant Mirror*
Meditate fifteen minutes
Buy "Gordon" and "Diesel #10" for Shane

The new approach not only gives me a different way of structuring my days, *but a different way of assessing them as well.* Previously, I had gone over my list at the end of my work-day, noting all the work-related tasks I had failed to accomplish and rescheduling them for the following day. Now, since all my activities serve the purpose of bringing harmony to my life, I review my day before I go to bed, attending to the breadth of things I have done. And so, without even intending to do so, I have seamlessly switched to a more positive way of assessing my daily achievements. Of course, I still often leave tasks undone, but this is now less important to me than ensuring that each day encompasses a broad cross section of activities.

Given the complexity of the demands of life in VUCA, however, *none* of us can hope to get everything done. This is a hard truth, and one it can take years to face. Yet acknowledging it offers a measure of freedom. For once we have accepted that finishing it all is an impossible aspiration, we can (like Chris Cappy) turn our attention to what we most *want* to do. And once we have clarified our real desires, we can be more conscious about choosing how we spend the hours that constitute our days.

The reason I was focusing my energies upon a single aspect of my life each day was a misguided belief that, by doing so, I could "clear my plate." That is, I imagined that once I had dealt with a particular set of tasks, I could remove them from my list and move on. I failed to understand that what I conceived of as "my plate" was in fact my life, and that *its very fullness was a measure of what lay at my core.* In an opportunity-rich environment that gives us the freedom to find our individual niches, identifying what lies at the core and finding ways to express it is the starting point for everything else.

4

Strategy Two:
Learn to Zigzag

"I guess I didn't follow the normal path."

Karen Van Dyke, the Internet marketer who asks her dreams to tell her what she needs to know, said this to me in the course of telling her story. She was hardly alone—virtually every person I interviewed stressed the singularity of his or her journey. They all said things such as *I didn't get here in the usual way. My career hasn't been conventional. I didn't take the typical route.*

Just what, I began to wonder, might qualify as the typical route, the conventional journey, the usual way, in our era? Nothing that I can readily imagine. We change jobs and careers with greater frequency and ease than in the past. This is in part because changes in technology and expanding globalization have made organizations far less stable, and in part because cheap and powerful personal computers have made us less dependent upon organizations to access the tools of work. We are also better educated, more well-traveled, and have a wider set of experiences than members of previous generations. All this has made us more independent in our thinking, and more likely to question traditional structures, institutions, and ways of working. There is also far less stigma attached to changing jobs. And so our individual paths have become increasingly idiosyncratic.

Just as our worklives are more varied, so also are our private lives. Some of us marry and start families early, some do so late, some have multiple marriages, some marry but choose not to have children, and a larger percentage of us live alone than in the past. There are single-parent families and blended families; single individuals adopt children; gay relationships are honored in commitment ceremonies. Couples can face the empty-nest syndrome in their late sixties or early forties. Retirement can come early or not at all. And, as the career counselor Judith Gerberg has pointed out, people today are likely to experience a "midlife crisis" while in their twenties.

The upshot of all this? There is no predetermined pattern to our lives anymore. There is no such thing as a neat and linear progression through a series of stages based upon age, as chronicled by Gail Sheehy in her early 1980s best-seller, *Passages: The Predictable Crises of Adult Life*. That book, still influential, appeared in the closing years of the industrial era, and the neat schema it presents ("The Breakaway Years," "The Deadline Decade") has little to do with how we live now.

Existence in today's VUCA environment does *not* proceed forward along a straight line. Rather, most of our lives seem to zigzag. Our early thirties may be the time for rethinking a long-cherished career choice; our late forties may find us back in school; our late fifties may find us dramatically changing our way of life, moving back into the city after twenty years away, trying our luck with a cattle ranch, or opening that antique shop we've always wanted.

Furthermore, our own zigzags don't look like anybody else's. Since life on the postindustrial frontier requires that we improvise to adapt to changing conditions, most of us are living through stages particular to *us,* rather than proceeding through life in lockstep with others of our generation.

We all know this. We see the evidence daily. We may have a boss who is fifteen years younger than we are. We may work with a team of five people who are all about the same age but each of whom has an entirely different life. Yet despite the proof that surrounds us, we often remain locked in a generic "passages" mind-set, internalizing the notion that we "should" be doing specific things (graduating from school, starting a family, being promoted, preparing for retirement) at specific times. Or we may imagine that we will be judged as lacking, or even as failures, if we do not reach an arbitrary point or attain a certain position by a given age, or if we don't weave the strands of our lives together in a particular way. We may even have bought the idea that we are too old to start over, too young to make a really big jump, or that the yearning for change we feel is simply the manifestation of a chronic discontent we should ignore so we can make peace with our circumstances.

We would be wrong to do this. For we would be depriving ourselves of one of the great advantages of living in a time of volatility, opportunity, and constant change.

The outdated notion that we "should" be moving through life in a particular way has become counterproductive. Arbitrary "time lines" (imagined as straight, moving irresistibly forward) now instead have the effect of holding us *back,* keeping us stuck by blinding us to opportunities that may not fit our expectations but might nevertheless lead in the direction we need to go.

It's not just our own assumptions that can cause us to misread our environment. All kinds of experts promote the "passages" idea. Executive recruiters, investment counselors, human resources managers, career guide advisers, and psychologists often tailor their advice based on schematic ideas about the stages of life. Nor does our educational system offer much help, since it was essentially designed to prepare people for life in the industrial era.

Sandy Alcorn, Chad Alcorn's mother and dean of the school of social work at Aurora University, just outside Chicago, sees the consequences of this disjunction. She says, "All the psychology and sociology textbooks available assume that life proceeds in predictable stages, or in accord with distinctive 'seasons.' This is no longer true, yet we continue to use these books in our classes because there's nothing else! But our students can't relate to what these books describe, especially the adult students. They all say, 'My life hasn't been like this! I didn't have my kids then! I don't view myself as being in that place.'" Sandy notes that "we've all become accustomed to thinking of these stages as deeply rooted in the human psyche. But in reality, they reflect the culture and the economics of any given time. And, as our students recognize, *everything* has changed during the last decade."

And so a key to thriving in today's environment is recognizing that the stages of life have changed. They are not set, but are rather malleable, individual, difficult to predict. Above all, they are dictated less by age than by opportunity and desire. This is good news, for it enables us to create a way of moving through life that satisfies what lies at our core and speaks to our specific needs. All of us can learn to zigzag, to recognize and embrace the crooked path we are already following.

We sacrifice some degree of security, yes. Few of us today can look forward to a retirement dinner capped by a presentation honoring forty years of loyal service. Few of us have the luxury of simply slotting into a position whose parameters have been clearly defined. The world we have left behind had its comforts and rewards, no doubt about it. But in leaving it, we have gained a great amount of freedom.

Yet freedom can be demanding. Life in our VUCA environment requires us not only to make more highly conscious choices, but also to continue to make them throughout our adult lives. This in turn challenges us to learn new ways of approaching work and life, as well as new skills.

What skills? What approaches? How do we adapt to such a free-flowing and open-ended environment? How do we get past the industrial-era legacy of generic life stages and begin designing ways of being that work for us as individuals? This chapter will examine five ways to embrace the world of zigzag:

- ❖ Learn from the youngest generation
- ❖ Think in terms of projects, engagements, gigs
- ❖ Plan to keep learning all your life
- ❖ Define what *you* mean by loyalty
- ❖ Internalize optimism

Learn from the youngest generation

The youngest generation of workers has a lot to teach us. Having grown up with computers and the Internet, they know in their bones just how drastically the rules have changed. As a result, they are improvising ways to shape careers and lives untethered from preordained stages, reflecting the reality of how work will be done in the future.

Of course, this generation is often criticized for its lack of loyalty. Its members are characterized as being "in it for themselves," having unrealistic expectations, being callow and opportunistic. Lucy Kellaway, a *Financial Times* columnist, typified this sentiment in a recent column when she chastised "spoilt twentysomethings" for expecting to be "empowered, cherished and stretched" at work, for believing that their jobs should fit *their* needs and satisfy their aspirations, rather than accepting the reality that *they* must adjust to the demands of their employers.

But Kellaway's tirade misses some important points. To begin with, it is difficult to imagine why the youngest workers would *not* expect to find work that fits their needs, since the whole message of our consumer society over the last two decades has been to "have it your way"—adapt whatever you want to your requirements, make it fit. Increasing customization, the practice of gearing products and services to ever more tightly defined niches, has been the guiding logic behind the economy for the past twenty-five years. Why then would it not also have become the guiding principle behind how people expect to work?

In addition, the economy in many parts of the developed

world has been expanding for more than a decade, giving younger people with desirable skills great negotiating power. Many point to this as the true reason that the new generation's expectations are unrealistic. As the economy suffers an inevitable downturn, they note, everything will change. This argument, of course, overlooks the fact that the *basis* of our economy has shifted, that organizations have become more dependent upon human knowledge and innovative ideas than in the past. This gives those who understand how the new system works greater power to shape their work to suit themselves.

Most important, criticizing younger people for holding unrealistic expectations overlooks the fact that their approach offers *all* of us a way to engage the future—especially when viewed without prejudice and with the recognition that the stages of life have changed. For the have-it-my-way attitude many younger workers display is above all a way of accommodating the instability that results from technological innovation and global markets.

Alicia Whitaker, a human resources executive at Pitney Bowes, has had plenty of opportunities to observe the approach that younger people bring. Her company, a one-hundred-year-old supplier of office systems based in Stamford, Connecticut, made a major commitment to developing a number of Internet businesses several years ago. As a result, Pitney Bowes has undertaken an aggressive effort to hire a good number of web-savvy people just a few years out of school. Doing so has had a dramatic impact upon its workplace culture.

Alicia explains: "Until the mid-1990s, our culture was very traditional. Many of our employees had never worked anywhere else. People tended to operate on the assumption that the *company* was responsible for shaping their careers—they admitted it freely when we questioned them about it. They expected the company to move them along, decide when it was time for them to make a change, all based upon what the company's needs were. In exchange for that level of security and dependence, our people were for the most part willing to work like slaves. Their whole mentality was, *it's about the company, I'm here to serve.*"

The younger people that Pitney Bowes began hiring have "just about the opposite attitude," says Alicia. "They see *themselves* as being in charge of their careers, and view the company's role as giving them a chance to develop their skills and broaden their relationships. They view their stint here as just that, *a stint,* a finite period of time that will enable them to move onto the next step. The questions they ask when I interview them reflect this. They want to know: How soon before I'm vested? Is the pension portable? What development opportunities will I have? What kind of skills will Pitney Bowes help me add to my portfolio? What I'm finding is that people from this generation will choose to work here—or not—based on how doing so adds to their value in the marketplace and enhances their lives."

Alicia notes that members of this generation are also very direct about their needs, which they have thought through in a highly deliberate way. "They'll tell you about how much community involvement they expect to have, what kind of flexibility they require, how they feel about travel, what their other interests are. They'll say, 'I'm not mobile now because I'm coaching soccer, but in four years or so I'll be able to go on the road.' They are totally life-style driven, clear about their priorities and boundaries. They're clear about their work being part of something larger—*their lives.*"

Of course, as Alicia points out, "This drives all of us in HR absolutely nuts! Our job has always been developing policies and procedures that treat people as *equals.* But that's out the window with the younger people. They don't care about policies, they want what works for *them.* And if we can't meet their demands, we are going to be screwed because we need their skills in order to compete in the Internet world. They know it, so they're forcing us to change. And setting a very good example for people my age, I might add. Because their attitude is absolutely appropriate, given the fact that no company on earth these days can promise that it will have a job for you in the future. Any company you can name might be in an entirely new business five years from now, and your skills might not fit. So you'll find the time has come to move *on.*"

It's a reality that must be absorbed by all of us. And one of the best ways to ensure that it will be is to make a practice of mixing with people of every age, so we can view things from the perspective of those with different experience. Much has been written over the last few years about the "war between the generations," the mutual resentment said to exist between baby boomers and youthful, tech-savvy hotshots who expect to be rewarded after just a few years on the job. I believe that, like the "war" between working women and stay-at-home mothers (most of whom are only temporarily at home), this conflict is largely a media-created battle. Still, it is common to find people on both sides of the age divide who undervalue the others' skills. Mixing socially and professionally only with people in one's own age group exacerbates such attitudes. Life in VUCA demands a far more open approach.

Think in terms of projects, engagements, gigs

Bonnie McEwan, director of communications for Planned Parenthood, employs large numbers of people directly out of college on her staff and also teaches nonprofit management at the New School for Social Research in New York City. She has thus had plenty of experience with younger workers, and she agrees with Alicia Whitaker that everyone can learn a lot from them.

Bonnie says, "People in their twenties are totally different than my generation, baby boomers in their forties and fifties. Most of the young people I have hired work hard and are very creative, but they absolutely work on their own terms. And you have to give them the freedom to do so or else they're *gone*. They don't see their careers unfolding in a linear way at all, as members of my generation did. It's more like they are living in the moment. They are primarily concerned with what they are doing and learning *now*."

Bonnie acknowledges that many people find such an approach to be shortsighted. But she does not believe it is, given the realities of our era. "I think younger people understand on a deep intuitive level how quickly things are changing because of the technology," she explains. "That's the real reason they take this approach. None of us can predict what work will be like in the future, or how people will relate to organizations. The situation is very fluid, and so are these younger workers. Some say it's flaky, but I say it makes a lot of sense."

Bonnie notes that the younger people she works with approach their work as a series of jobs or engagements. "*Gigs,* really, as if they were in a band. They often use that term. There's something provisional about their approach." Alicia Whitaker concurs. "When we conduct interviews with younger candidates, they'll tell us, for example, 'I want to work on the development of imaging products because that's a skill I'll probably need in the future.' They don't envision themselves as wanting to *be* in imaging, they don't think of imaging as their long-term career, because who knows what this business will look like in ten years? No. They decide that imaging is a field they need to learn about, and they then set about finding work that will help them to do that." From the way managers like Alicia and Bonnie describe it, younger people today think of their jobs as *classes* or workshops, in which they can learn essential skills.

Bonnie adds a further observation. "With a lot of the younger people I hire, there's not much of a dividing line between the gigs they do for money and the gigs they do for fun. In a very original way, they see it as all part of the same thing, aspects of their lives that express their different interests. This can be confusing; it's totally uncompartmentalized, untraditional. It's not like the old volunteer work that people did on the side, either as a way of networking or in order to make a contribution."

Aliza Sherman, a website designer in her twenties, exemplifies this trend. She says, "I don't really see my work as separate from how I spend my spare time or have fun or learn about the world. It's all the same thing, really. I mean, what is work? It's just the way you express yourself and create an identity. Whether or not you get paid for it isn't the main thing. Of course, your work has to support you, you have to figure out how to make it pay. But that's not *why* you do it. You do it because you need to express yourself in the world. And lots of activities give you ways to do that."

Perhaps because Aliza sees work as inextricable from identity, she integrates her gigs in the way that Bonnie McEwan describes. Aliza says, "When I put up my first website, I didn't use a photograph. I drew a cartoon character and called her Cybergrrl. I saw her as a kind of superheroine of the Internet. At the same time, she was also me. So whatever I'm doing, it's about Cybergrrl—new learning for her, new friends or connections, new plans and projects."

Bonnie McEwan notes a similar attitude in regard to her younger employees' personal relationships. "They don't see them as being separate from their work. Instead, their work and their friends are part of a larger whole." This can manifest itself in surprising ways. "I've had times when I've walked into a younger employee's office, and found two of his friends just hanging out—people who don't even work here! And part of me wants to say, *time to get to work!* But another part of me has learned to recognize that whatever is going on may very well turn out to have a positive outcome for the organization."

Bonnie cites an example. "We had a young woman who ran our college action programs. She did a great job, was very imaginative and hardworking, and she seemed to know everyone, which was useful. For some reason, she had a lot of friends in the music business, and they would come to our events. I would see them around, sometimes just hanging out, sometimes helping. They weren't being paid, but they weren't formal volunteers. Then suddenly one spring, this young woman announced that she was going to leave her job for a few months so that she could go on tour with the music festival *Lilith Fair*. She *thought* she wanted to come back to work for us later, but wasn't sure. In any case, this is what she wanted to do right *now*. We were upset because we assumed it meant we would lose her. We could hardly promise her job would be waiting when—and if—she decided to return. But it just turned out to be a change in our relationship with her. While she was on tour, she'd set up Planned Parenthood tables at concerts, and get people with the band to staff them. She wasn't working *for* us, it was just something she did, a way of bringing two of her interests together. Plus she began helping us get all these well-known musicians to do our events—people we would have had a hard time reaching. It was like some brilliant marketing plan, only it wasn't a marketing plan. It was just her going about her life in the way *she* wanted and making great things happen for us in the process. It was just her having a couple of different gigs."

Bonnie had a similar experience with one of the webmasters she hired. "She did great work, but she decided to go back to school and get an advanced degree in web design. We figured we wouldn't see her again. But as soon as she started school, she began recruiting friends in the program to write and edit things for our website. They did it as part of their course work. So we suddenly had this whole team of grad students working on our website, and it became incredibly exciting. Again, we could have come up with an elaborate Internet plan and spent a lot of money on development. But instead she took the initiative and made stuff happen, because it happened to fit with what *she* wanted to do at the time."

Jim Treyz, head of global sales for Citibank, employs large numbers of younger people all over the world. He too notices their tendency to conceive of employment, even at a well-paying global powerhouse like Citibank, as a series of temporary engagements, and believes we all have a lot to learn from it.

Jim says, "I take strong issue with this notion that the younger people in the workplace have no sense of commitment. On the contrary, I find them very committed. But their commitment is to *a much shorter time horizon.* They take a job primarily for the experience, for what they can learn. And one thing is certain—they're not interested in toughing it out under a bad manager! There's much more an idea of freedom, of empowerment, of the individual using the organization to meet his or her personal goals. Even five years ago, an MBA would ask his or her manager, 'Where am I going in this company? How do I get there? What do you have planned for me?' Well, you don't hear that anymore. Now it's, 'Let me tell you where I'm going. Let me lay out what's of interest to me. Let me inform you what I plan to accomplish in the time I have here.' It's a totally self-directed approach, and it's kind of startling when you're a manager. But it's highly adaptive when the organization is in flux."

Bonnie McEwan takes Jim's observations one step further: "What I see developing is really an *entirely* new way of working. It's not about building a career in the traditional sense. That's what my generation did, that was how we approached things. But when you think in terms of career building, you get invested in having things go a certain way. You follow a particular path so you can reach long-term goals. And if you can't keep to that path or reach those goals, you tend to get derailed, feel betrayed, or you wonder where you've failed. But when everything is constantly changing, in both the for-profit and nonprofit worlds, things *can't* be expected to go according to plan. That's what the younger people I work with seem totally to understand. So they take a more experimental, open-ended approach. They improvise their careers based on what seems useful or interesting at the time. If one thing doesn't pan out, they'll try something else, without getting all wrought up about it."

Approaching work as a series of projects is not just for younger people, of course. Barbara Roberts, the CEO of Acoustiguide, has always taken this view. She says, "I've never believed in long-range planning for anything except finances and health. All those five- and ten-year career plans people come up with rarely succeed because they're based on projecting the present into the future. Things are changing much too fast for that. How can we know the future? Who knows what the impact of the Internet is ultimately going to be? I think long-range plans are also a problem because they encourage you to think about your life in terms of stages, or in terms of what other people expect. What you want is a life that is integrated, rich, and whole, and allows you to express all the different parts of yourself—not one governed by artificial deadlines that have to do with outward measures of success."

Plan to keep learning all your life

Thinking in terms of gigs not only acknowledges the unstable realities of life in VUCA, it also serves as a tool for breaking down the old industrial era divide between learning and work.

The industrial era viewed life as divided into three separate, distinct, and highly predictable periods: education, work, and retirement. Work—a career with a predictable arc during which one was continually employed—spanned the long period between the years spent in school and the years when one no longer earned a living. Work was not *itself* about learning; instead, it gave individuals a chance to apply what they had been taught.

This highly compartmentalized approach does not come close to meeting the demands of the knowledge era.

Today, the currency each of us has in an open market is determined by the breadth, depth, and up-to-dateness of what we know, and by the extent to which we ourselves take responsibility for our learning. Under the old system, our learning was provided for us—by parents, by the government, by the organizations for which we worked. They determined the parameters of what we needed to know, and they determined how and when we should know it. Learning itself was industrialized, cut so that one size would fit all, starting in grade school and continuing on through the generic management-training programs offered by large companies.

All this has now been turned on its head. Each of us needs to determine for ourselves the course, content, method, outcome, and setting of our individual learning. Each of us needs to put together a customized program from among the countless offerings that are available to us—colleges and universities, technical-training institutes, weekend workshops and seminars, distance-learning programs. We can also benefit enormously and expand our expertise by offering ourselves as apprentices to people from whom we believe we have a lot to learn.

Julie Anixter, vice president of development and new media for the legendary writer and business guru Tom Peters, has a long history of doing just that. Several years ago, when she was director of training at a large corporation outside Chicago, Julie became intrigued by an interactive learning software called the ASK System, which had been developed at Northwestern University. The ASK System permits the user to train himself or herself by providing specific answers to a range of questions. It has been used by the U.S. military to teach logistical supply and by high schools to teach history. It's a smart software that permits a high degree of customization, and Julie thought her company should adopt it. But she also decided she wanted to become an expert on the ASK technology herself.

So Julie adjusted the parameters of her job so she could spend as much time as possible at the learning lab where the ASK system had been developed. On the one hand, she was checking out its usefulness for her company, which did indeed end up buying it. On the other hand, she was serving an informal apprenticeship at the lab. "I wanted to soak up everything I could from the brilliant people who had developed the system. Basically, I just wanted to be around them! I wanted to study the technology, yes, but I also wanted to see what it meant in terms of learning, in terms of the many ways it could be applied." Julie spent so much time at the lab that she ended up matriculating for a master's degree at Northwestern, designing her course work in conjunction with the lab.

Of course, returning to a bricks-and-mortar institution is no longer a necessary first step in integrating new learning into our work. The Internet is an extraordinary resource that enables us to create highly specific, inexpensive learning programs for ourselves. Distance-learning organizations such as the University of Phoenix, Union Graduate Center in Cincinnati, and the California Institute of Integral Studies offer a wide range of learning sent over the Internet to user groups. We are truly at the beginning of a revolution in what was formerly institutionalized as "education." It is fascinating to witness how both the *obligation* and the *resources* to create our own ways and means of learning are shifting to us as individuals at the same time.

The need to keep learning throughout the entire span of our adult lives, rather than trying to jam our learning into the early years of adulthood, has great implications for how we spend our resources.

If we are young and just starting our career, we might decide not to assume the heavy debt required for a traditional four-years-away at college, but to attend a school closer to home, saving our money so we can return to classes after we've had some work experience.

If we are in mid-career and feel stuck or threatened by instability, we might decide to sacrifice a major acquisition that our income suggests we can afford and instead pursue a second degree. Such a degree could not only better position us in the market but could also enable us to start over in a completely new field that is more appealing to the person we have become.

If we are nearing the age that used to automatically signal retirement, we might begin to pursue training we need to embark upon a late-life career in some new arena that has begun to interest us, rather than earmarking those funds for retirement.

The need for continuous learning requires that we find ways to integrate our work with our learning, to learn from our work even as we work at our learning. This means that we must analyze each project that we choose to undertake in terms of the opportunities it presents to expand what we know. The youthful hires whom Alicia Whitaker and Jim Treyz interviewed were doing just this when they questioned their prospective employees about how what they learned on the job would increase their own value. They were looking at work itself as a means, and an instrument, of learning.

Here again, approaching our careers as a series of engagements or gigs can be helpful. The concept of a *gig* comes from the world of jazz. A musical gig is the perfect example of a project. It takes place within a specific and limited time frame; it brings together a group that may or may not have worked together before and may or may not work together again; it offers members of the group a chance to learn from one another; it is open-ended in terms of possibilities for the future. It is *work*, but it functions as a *workshop*.

Even time spent away from work, during a sabbatical or in a period between jobs, can be approached in a way that ultimately adds to our knowledge, our experience, our relationships, and thus our value. New York career counselor Judith Gerberg has noticed an upsurge of mid-career men and women who have become interested in serving stints in the Peace Corps. She says, "It used to be something people did *before* starting their careers, after college. The idea of taking two years off from work in mid-life was just unheard of. But now, people in their thirties, forties, fifties and beyond are bringing their experience, in medicine or teaching or logistics, to parts of the world in need of help. Maybe these people feel the need to do something meaningful, or maybe they just want to be immersed in a different culture and escape their particular rut. In any case, while this kind of service is extremely satisfying in terms of enabling us to make a contribution, it's also a great way for people to learn new skills that they can apply later on."

Sharon Capeling-Alakija, global director of United Nations Volunteers, has witnessed something similar: a dramatic rise in year-long volunteerships among working adults with high-level accounting, financial, and computer skills. "These are the skills that countries trying to build sustainable infrastructure most need," she points out. "And experienced people are more eager to supply them. The great advantage doing a UN volunteership today is that it provides you with the chance to apply your skills in a global environment. That adds to your base of knowledge and experience, gives you a whole lot of new contacts, and has the end effect of making you more valuable."

Expanding the range of our learning is also a way of positioning ourselves for whatever we decide we want to do *next* in our lives. It is a way of building a career based on skills we have mastered rather than positions we have filled. The old hierarchical approach to career building usually required us to serve as an underling to a more senior person who did *not* share his knowledge or his skills. After doing so, we were promoted into a more senior position simply because we had served our time.

Careers in hierarchical organizations thus depended upon the existence of predictable rungs by which people could ascend. Those who failed to ascend usually had to leave, the industrial-era corporate mantra being "up or out."

But we can no longer assume that the rungs "above" us will even exist in five years, given the rush to flatten organizations. Nor can we assume that the skills of those who hold high positions will necessarily be the ones we will need even a year or two from now. And so, the time-serving approach to career building has become pointless and increasingly obsolete. As Ellen (Lin) Knapp, vice chair and chief information officer of PricewaterhouseCoopers, notes, "What matters today is what you know and how up-to-date your thinking is, not where you've been positioned on the ladder."

Lin Knapp also notes that today's emphasis on continuous learning has become a powerful means of eroding stereotypes about age that have long existed in organizations. She says, "We're coming full circle on the gray hair issue now. Experienced people are being seen as very valuable, because value is more and more defined on the basis of what you know. We're also starting to realize that people provide value *along a continuum,* contributing different skills and attitudes and talents at different ages. This means that the most effective teams are those that embrace a range of skills and ages, instead of those that group people according to their level."

Lin cites a *Business Week* survey in which nearly 30 percent of younger CEOs reported that their companies' ability to grow was limited by their *own* lack of managerial skills. "Companies today need people who know how to manage, people who've been around and have broad contacts and solid reputations. Plus they need the savvy younger people who are comfortable with the technology and understand how it is morphing whatever industry they are in. It's not like the old hierarchy, where it was assumed that the top person was responsible for the success of an effort. Things are too complicated, there is just too much to *know*. Work gets done by teams, so there's a more network-centric approach." Lin therefore advises those who want to succeed in this environment "to see whatever team you're part of as a *system*. You need to figure out what the system is, how it functions, how the parts fit together, what it needs, where it should be going. Once you understand that, you can then determine what *you* have to contribute. And that in turn will tell you what you need to know, where you need to expand your knowledge."

Define what *you* mean by loyalty

There's been a great deal of agonizing about the disappearance of loyalty over the last decade or so. We hear how organizations are no longer loyal to their employees, how employees are no longer loyal to their companies. We bemoan the demise of team loyalty among professional athletes. We wonder whatever happened to party loyalty in politics. We note the dwindling sense of loyalty people have to the communities they live in, and move out of with increasing frequency. Altogether, we give ourselves a bad rap on the loyalty front.

But perhaps it's really our *definition* of loyalty that's changing, in response to fast-changing conditions. To begin with, much of the loyalty that employees and companies are said to have felt for one another in the late industrial era was based on the kind of paternalism that Alicia Whitaker describes among the older workers at Pitney Bowes. People depended upon large organizations because they had little choice but to work for them, since the means of producing and distributing most products and services were too large and expensive for individuals to own or control. What we now call loyalty when we speak of the past was thus the direct result of people's wholly appropriate self-interest.

In addition, loyalty used to reflect the fact that relationships between people and organizations were clearly defined. You either worked for a company or you did not. Organizations did not have porous membranes. They rarely subcontracted work out. Nor did they rely upon a loosely defined network of suppliers, partners, and independent workers, as is so often the case today. People were loyal in part because they knew precisely where they stood.

The traditional view of loyalty—which might indeed be summarized as *the company knows best*— began to erode in the late 1960s. Before that, companies had routinely shifted their male executives around between far-flung offices without regard for their private lives. But once women began working, such transfers became problematic, and soon newspapers were heralding previously unheard-of instances of men actually leaving their jobs rather than agreeing to yet another move.

By the late 1970s, the forces of globalization had begun to take hold, and organizations became more unstable and vulnerable to competition. As a result, they began laying people off, contracting out a broad range of functions, and adapting new technologies to operate more leanly. People displaced after years of loyal service were outraged by the betrayal of what had seemed to them an almost sacred trust, *yet their trust had always been misplaced.* For it was based on the presumption that their employers would always have a place for them—which was in turn based on a belief that their employers had the ability to control, or at least to predict, their markets.

So where does all this leave us?

Is everyone "just in it for themselves" these days, as so many maintain? Perhaps so, but it seems more realistic to conclude that our attitude toward loyalty (at least as it is exists in the workplace) is healthier than it was in the industrial era. We now understand—or should—that we must rely first upon ourselves. And we have begun to build our lives based on that awareness.

The upshot is that we get to define *for ourselves* where our loyalties lie. Bill Taylor, publisher of *Fast Company* magazine, often considered the new bible of people in the workplace, has an interesting take on how loyalty is manifest today. He says, "I think the whole definition of loyalty has changed. People aren't loyal to letterhead or laundry any more. They're loyal to what they're trying to accomplish in the world, to what they see as their purpose. That means they are loyal to whatever it is they are trying to *design,* loyal to the individuals or team they are directly involved with. You hear it all the time, people say, 'I care about the people I work with, *they* are the company to me.' Or they are loyal to a certain *way* of working, or even a technology. When someone says, 'I'm loyal to Mac,' it's not the name that they're loyal to, it's the *process,* what the Mac enables them to do. Or they might feel very invested in the *way* they manage people in their organization. They think of these things as part of their identity, part of what they are trying to create. *That's* the key. Loyalty has more to do with individual identity, what you're offering to the world, and less to do with affiliation."

Such an approach to work is similar to that traditionally taken by artists, who are both highly self-directed and likely to feel a primary loyalty to the methods and materials they use. Most artists, indeed, find their individual style *at the same time* that they discover "their" materials, during a period of apprenticeship and searching. Picasso found his identity and began a revolution in art when he started using collage, incorporating bits of fabric, newspaper, string, and twigs into his paintings in a way that no one had ever done before. Jackson Pollock established his distinctive "drip" style when he found his signature medium—ready-mixed common housepaint made from enamel and aluminum, which enabled him to spin a network of loops and whorls onto a flat canvas. Mies van der Rohe began creating the modernist buildings for which he became known when he discovered how to use corten steel together with glass to make an entirely new and open kind of structure.

This sort of merging of individual identity with specific techniques and materials is now occurring in many arenas outside the arts.

It is apparent in declarations such as *I'm loyal to Java* or *What I care about most is building a more weblike and inclusive team.* Such statements are evidence of a widespread evolution to more artful, individualistic, mature, and ultimately satisfying definitions of loyalty.

There are many ways for people today to create a distinct offering to the world. But crafting an offer requires that you both understand and define exactly what *you* are loyal to.

Taking the time to think this through can also be a powerful means for gaining greater clarity about who you are and what you really want to do. To this end, you need to ask yourself some questions:

- Who are the people you feel most loyal to?
- What ideas do you want to promote in the world?
- What tool do you prize using above all others?
- Do you enjoy working on several things at once or on sequential projects?
- Do you prefer working on a project alone or with a team?
- Do you like mapping out where you're going or stumbling upon it?
- In what areas is your intuition sharpest?
- What medium best enables you to express yourself? Is it words? images? music? games? food? clothing? wood? auto engines? software? flowers? logistical systems? marketing plans? political campaigns? Or is your true medium *people?*

Asking such questions in an attempt to define your loyalties also serves as a means of connecting to your core, for your loyalties reveal a lot about your values.

Internalize optimism

Frontier eras such as ours have always both demanded and rewarded optimism, for it takes faith to move forward in uncertain times. And it requires a positive view of the world to master unsettled conditions. And so optimism—the virtue and spur of the pioneer—is absolutely key to thriving in 24/7. Optimism breeds confidence, and we need to be confident if we are to negotiate our individual yet changing needs from a position of strength. Optimism also inspires buoyancy, and we must be buoyant if we are to move beyond stereotypes about where we should be and what we should be doing at a given age.

The confidence and optimism many younger workers feel probably goes a long way toward explaining why they have proven adept at managing life in VUCA. Throughout most of history, of course, young people have been optimistic and buoyant, convinced that they will be able to change the world and make it better. But the generation that has come of age as the millennium has turned seems to hold a particular advantage. Having grown up not only during a boom, but *during a boom that has particularly rewarded individual entrepreneurs and investors,* has perhaps given them a special faith in their ability to have and do what it takes.

As Bonnie McEwan at Planned Parenthood observes,

> A lot of the younger people I work with seem to have this incredible belief in their skills and their value. So they tend to be fearless, to feel as if they just walk away if something doesn't suit them. To me, this indicates a pretty benign picture of how the universe operates. And I think that's ultimately the key to their success. My generation—the first wave of the baby boomers—simply did not grow up with this attitude. We were confident about our ability to change social

conditions and make the world a better place, but we weren't all that confident about risks when it came to work. Our parents lived through the Depression and tended to have more of a scarcity mentality. They instilled in us the idea that we're lucky if we just have a job. And then of course there was such a shortage of jobs in the early seventies, with Ph.D.s driving cabs and that sort of thing, that I don't think most of us ever really internalized the idea that the workplace would adapt to meet our needs. So a lot of us have this inappropriate fear of letting our companies know what we want or expect. It's an attitude that leads to a lot of stress and overwork.

Barbara Grogan, the founder and CEO of Western Industrial Contractors, a construction company based in Denver, spends many days each month talking to M.B.A. students, and she agrees with Bonnie's observation. "What's happening today is the most incredible instance of opportunity meeting preparedness," she says. "By that I mean, this generation that is *precisely* right for today's conditions. The people I meet in their twenties have this attitude that the world is their oyster. They see no boundaries in terms of what they can be and do. I think this has to do with their being intensely in touch with their needs. Being in touch with your needs is essential in a time when everything is changing very fast. There's no way to keep up, so you just have to focus on what you need, what you want to do, what you have to contribute."

●　●　●

If optimism and confidence are key to taming the new world of work, *what do you do if you're not all that optimistic?*

What do you do if you're having trouble getting past the scarcity approach? What if you seem hardwired to notice only the negatives? What if fears about the future sometimes threaten to overwhelm you? What if life appears to you to be getting worse instead of better?

If you're not an optimist, should you just give up and wallow in your sense of doom?

Not at all. There are concrete steps that each of us can take to triumph over pessimism and doubt.

First, we need to uncover and confront the negative messages we may have grown up with and internalized. These include:

- "You're lucky just to have a job."
- "Who are *you* to get precisely what you want?"
- "Don't set yourself above other people—it's dangerous."
- "Don't set yourself above your family—it's disloyal."
- "Life is tough, get used to it."

Identifying and uprooting such messages requires persistence and courage because such messages are acquired very early. We may have become so accustomed to living with these assumptions that we feel they lie at the root of our identity. If we were to let go of our fears, we wouldn't recognize ourselves. In addition, because such messages are usually instilled in us by our family of origin, questioning them can seem to set us against our parents.

As psychologist Stanley Siegel points out, "Large numbers

of people out there today are carrying around messages from their families regarding work and ambition that are *totally* at odds with today's environment. Often they know these messages are hindering them, but they feel that letting go of them would show disloyalty to their families. In fact, they *prove* their loyalty by carrying these messages around! It's one of the major reasons that people are reluctant to let them go." Siegel notes that combating such internalized beliefs requires a lot of work, which is usually most effectively done with a therapist, a career counselor, or a coach.

Second, we need to start *acting* as if we are positive and optimistic.

An increasing amount of research suggests that simply behaving in a particular way sets in motion a whole series of physiological changes in the body that transform the act into reality. This is because the neurotransmitters in our brains respond to physical signals, setting off chemical changes that in turn affect our feelings. And so emotions manifested on the outside are likely to move inward *simply because they are physically expressed.*

For example, in one study, a group of depressed individuals was instructed to smile every two minutes—at another person, at themselves in the mirror, or even at a chair or a door if that's what presented itself. Immediately, every participant began to register brain wave changes that indicated a more positive and hopeful attitude. In another study, people were paired with individuals they disliked and with whom they disagreed. They were then instructed to nod their heads in agreement with each point their adversary made. After an hour in one another's company, every respondent reported liking the individual with whom they were paired better than they had in the past, and to have greater tolerance for and understanding of his or her point of view. In other words, people tended to feel agreeable because they smiled, rather than smiling because they felt agreeable.

Such research suggests that, to *be* optimistic, we first need to *act* optimistic, coaxing forth positive feelings rather than waiting for them to develop within us. This means working to eliminate the negative commentary that so often goes on inside our heads: *I can't afford to trust people; of course the plane will be late and I'll miss my connection; whatever can go wrong almost certainly will.*

But coaxing forth positive feelings also means refusing to communicate with others on the basis of petty complaint—bitterly detailing our struggles with the phone company, railing against the idiotic salesperson who got our order wrong, enumerating the faults of our boss. And it means refusing to be drawn into gripe sessions with people who've simply acquired the habit of complaining. Instead, we need to find ways to turn such conversations in a positive direction, or make an effort to avoid such people as often as we can.

In addition, we need to smile, recognizing and believing that this simple act has an extraordinary power, both to lift our own spirits and to inspire those around us. We need to deliberately meditate upon what is good in our lives. We need to count our blessings, even at those moments when we're not feeling particularly grateful. And we need to understand that optimism isn't something given out to certain lucky people at birth, but is instead a habitual way of thinking and reacting that every one of us can acquire. We need to trust that our own actions and thoughts can impact our brain chemistry in such a way that we can become profoundly hopeful and more at peace.

Finally, we must focus on specific ways we can address the problems of life on the postindustrial frontier, rather than simply lamenting the negative aspects of the world in which we find ourselves.

The VUCA environment is not a particularly comfortable place. Amid good fortune and much prosperity, people *are* being left behind, either because they do not have the skills that the economy values or because their circumstances—medical problems, unstable families—make the effort of keeping up too much of a strain. The generally rising tide is *not* lifting all boats, and the gap between rich and poor is growing. Those who maintain that free markets alone can redress all inequities are not facing the complex reality of the world we live in.

The primary problem is that we are living through a time of major transition. The old support systems that helped protect people from the brutalities of the marketplace—everything from settlement houses to federal welfare programs to large labor unions—were crafted to meet the needs of the industrial economy. These institutions have proven unequal to the demands of the knowledge economy, in which one-size-fits-all solutions are often ineffective. As a result, the old supports have been abandoned as obsolete, lumbering, and unnecessarily bureaucratic, leaving us with fewer institutions to protect those with the least resources.

Building appropriate new institutions of support will be the work of the next few decades. Each one of us has the potential to make a contribution to this effort. Understanding the root of the problem (economic transition) and finding concrete ways to work to relieve the suffering it causes and give people greater access to resources is a reasonable and constructive approach to the problem. Certainly, this is a more effective approach than denouncing the changes technology has wrought or feeling depressed about society's direction.

It is also an approach that actually *produces* greater optimism. Research indicates that people who work to alleviate the suffering of others are happier and more positive than the general population; this is true even of those who work with the terminally ill. Such people are probably more keenly aware of their own blessings, of the fragile nature of life, and are thus more likely to dwell on the gratitude they feel. Rather than "comparing up," judging their own circumstances by contrasting them with those more favored (easy to do in a prosperous time), they are more likely to "compare down," contrasting their own situations with those who are less fortunate. Comparing up has always been a recipe for unhappiness as those of us who have done it can attest.

Internalizing optimism does not mean becoming a Pollyanna, someone who ignores reality in favor of a relentlessly rosy view. It does mean understanding that a positive approach is absolutely within our grasp and working to cultivate it. For our fast-changing world is rich with opportunity, but it's hard to *see* opportunity when you're focused on the negative.

5

Strategy Three:
Create Your Own Work
(Even If You Stay in Your Job)

Given the intensity of life in 24/7, we cannot really enjoy our days if we have no control over our work, if we are at the beck and call of a boss who expects too much, or if our company fails to respect our contribution. Nor can our lives be fully satisfying if we feel creatively muzzled, or are stuck doing work that does not allow us to express our talents.

If we feel overworked, undervalued, stifled, or otherwise misused, we have three alternatives:

We can remain in an unsatisfying situation and tell ourselves that we are simply doing our duty—being prudent, supporting loved ones, demonstrating loyalty.

We can leave our organization and search for an entirely new job.

Or we can figure out how to adapt our present job to better reflect our interests and our needs, thus creating a partnership with our employer rather than a "working for" arrangement.

The problem with the first approach is not only that it is soul-destroying. It is also ultimately a losing game. Trying to fit in, attempting to adjust our expectations to meet what we believe our company wants from us, might have been an asset in the old industrial economy, when loyalty was highly valued. But today's knowledge economy rewards individuality, originality, innovation, and boldness. In such an environment, organizations are not eager to hold onto people who are content to muddle through.

Thus, stifling ourselves to try to live out someone else's vision of what we "should" be doing makes it less likely that we will succeed. And so our willingness to compromise, far from proving our adaptability, has the effect of identifying us as a low-value employee.

The second approach, leaving the company, has proven popular over the last decade; the 1990s saw the highest quit rate in history. Many people profiled in this book have moved from one organization to another in an effort to find the right fit for their talents, or to pursue new interests that developed as they explored their inner core. Most of these individuals concluded that the kind of work they were doing was wrong for them, given their true passions and skills. Or they felt that the culture in which they were working clashed with their own particular style.

But quitting a job is not always practical, given the complex realities of our lives. Our husband may have just returned to school, our wife may be starting a new career, we may be supporting two kids in college. In addition, moving onto the next thing doesn't guarantee that we'll find a better situation, especially given the volatility of today's environment. One woman I spoke with had left an important retail position to take a job with an international clothing company known for its creative culture. "I felt I needed a more artistic environment," she explained. Two months after her move, the company's European headquarters decided to phase out the line she'd been hired to direct because the parent firm had bought a big mass-market label and wanted to switch its focus to something less upscale. So she's out looking for a job.

Trying to adapt our present work to better reflect our interests (the third approach) avoids the either/or, all-or-nothing conundrum. It requires us neither to compromise our values to stay in our present position nor to search for something entirely new. It is instead a means of finding balance between what *we* want from life and what our organization needs.

It is also an alternative that has been open to very few until recent years. The balance of power in the industrial era rested firmly on the side of organizations. Individuals had little scope to affect the shape or workings of their companies unless they managed to achieve the top position. But it is becoming easier for us today to affect the kind of work our organizations do, and to devise more satisfactory ways of working in the process.

Why is this so?

To begin with, many companies, seeking to operate more leanly, have decentralized decision-making. Nurses prepare care plans and patient schedules. Engineers have a say in how their designs are marketed. Librarians choose the technology that enables patrons to access information. Sales teams set their own goals for the year ahead.

In addition, the kind of top-down strategic planning that dominated organizations in the seventies and eighties has become obsolete. Elaborate formal plans devised by strategic specialists have proven too distant from frontline and marketplace reality to work in our VUCA world. At the same time, innovation has become far more important because product cycles move so fast. So organizations have begun looking for innovators in the ranks: teachers who devise new ways to deliver courses, financial planners who identify fresh markets, store managers who suggest new product lines.

As a result, decisions that used to land on the chairman's desk are now made in operating units, and companies are taking increasing advantage of the ideas raised by employees.

This evolution in the world of work gives most of us more power—*power that isn't necessarily linked to our position.* As career counselor Judith Gerberg points out, "Companies are more fluid than they used to be. More and more, they take their shape from the people who work within them, rather than imposing their shape and structure upon their people."

The fact that so many organizations at least recognize that they must take their shape from us (even if our company hasn't quite figured out how to do it!) makes it easier for us to carve out fresh and individual ways of working within them. The trick is finding a way to mesh our needs with our companies' long-term mission.

Tailoring your work to meet your needs without leaving your organization requires skill, planning, even cunning. If this is your choice, there are specific steps you need to take. You need to figure out a way to:

❖ Articulate your value
❖ Integrate your passions
❖ Identify your market
❖ Run your own shop
❖ Target multiple centers of gravity

Articulate your value

Creating your own work in partnership with an organization requires confidence and negotiating skills, for you need to be able to make your case to the company that employs you. Both confidence and the ability to negotiate derive from a firm understanding of what you have to offer and the ability to articulate it well.

Judith Gerberg's job is to help people to do this. She says, "If you want to create your own work, you must start by being very clear about your value. No one will see you as valuable unless you see yourself that way. And unless you make a strong case for what you have to offer."

The sequence goes like this:

- You need to know precisely what you bring to the table
- You need to be able to enumerate your advantages in a forceful way
- You need to make a persuasive case about how your organization can benefit from making better use of your skills

How do you go about doing these things? Judith Gerberg says that the foundation is understanding what you have to offer. She suggests that you begin by making a list of your skills, both specific and general. The list should include:

- Your computer skills—the programs and operating systems you have mastered
- Your people skills—how you manage, how you operate on a team

- Your ability to make speeches or presentations in public
- Your knowledge and understanding of customers and markets
- Your ability to promote ideas you believe in
- Your values and beliefs about your work
- Your professional network
- Your associations outside your profession
- The expertise you've acquired in school and in professional development programs
- Your interests, passions, particular talents
- Global qualifications, such as foreign languages

Once you have compiled a comprehensive list of what you have to offer, it's up to you to enumerate those advantages in a forceful way, drawing the attention of potential allies in your company to the range of your skills.

Sometimes we feel awkward about doing this. We fear we will be perceived as blowing our own horn, bragging or boasting in an unbecoming way. Or we feel our talents should be recognized without our having to point them out. This would be nice, but it rarely happens. If showcasing your own talents and achievements is a problem for you, you need to find ways of doing so that don't violate your personal comfort zone.

Take, for example, Ellen Isaacs. Ellen was developing training programs for engineers at Sun Microsystems when I met her several years ago. She was in her late twenties, and had a strong sense of what she brought to the organization. But she wasn't particularly skilled at making it known. A performance review from her boss brought this home to her. "He wrote that I was an excellent worker, but said I stayed too much in my shell, didn't get around the company enough. Well, I couldn't have been more surprised! I'm very much a go-to person; people all over the company are always dropping into my office to talk, e-mailing me with problems and questions. I have a strong, solid network, and always felt it was a great asset to me. And here I was being perceived of as isolated and standoffish!"

Ellen wondered what she had failed to do.

"The more I thought about it," she said, "the more I realized the problem. *I* knew about my network, but I hadn't bothered to let my boss know! I just took it for granted he would see me in a certain way. So I simply began dropping into his office on a regular basis to let him know who I had talked to that day, or sending a short e-mail about it. It was very casual, informal, and at first I was afraid he would think I was wasting his time or bragging. But I soon discovered just the opposite was true. He *wanted* to know what I was doing, because it indicated to him that his department was on top of things, that we were at the center of decision-making. He saw my being in touch with a lot of people as strengthening *him,* not as me just blowing my own horn. This taught me how important it is to showcase my talents, instead of just expecting that people will recognize what I do best."

Judith Gerberg suggests that, once we have taken an inventory of our skills and talents, we should write a résumé based upon what we have discovered. "Don't focus on jobs or titles that you've held," she advises. "Focus upon what you *know,* what you have done, what you've learned. Be as concrete as you can. Above all, give a flavor for who you *are*." Most of us, Gerberg notes, prepare our résumés when we are about to look for a new job. Your purpose in writing this résumé is to vouch for your own preparedness so that you can begin to shift the nature of your present work.

Julie Anixter, vice president for new media for Tom Peters, has a history of a creating her own work inside organizations, as we saw in Chapter 4. She believes her ability to articulate and draw attention to her individual talents is the primary reason she has been successful in this effort.

Julie says, "I think the reason I've been able to persuade the companies I've worked with to let me develop projects that reflect my own passions is that I am very clear about demonstrating what I bring. I know my value. I'm a big-picture person. I read the world broadly. I'm good at synthesizing big ideas and then designing training, conferences and events in a way that's dramatic and compelling. I'm good at creating memorable experiences for people. I have a great appreciation for the theater. I have a background in design. These are the kinds of things I put in my résumé, *not* a list of qualifications and previously held jobs. My résumé is about the direction I want to go, so I use it internally, to keep people aware of what I bring. And of course, to remind myself!"

Using a résumé is useful because it serves as a tool to help you find a fit between what you are qualified to do, what you would like to do, and an arena that might be of future benefit to your organization. *It does not matter if your organization is not at present engaged in the kind of work you have in mind.* It is important only that you be able to articulate why pursuing a particular line of activity would further the company's overall mission. Then you need to design a project that reflects your interests, and lobby to head it up.

Julie Anixter has done this a number of times, most notably in her previous job, when she persuaded her company to incorporate the ASK System into its training program. Julie did this in part because she believed that the ASK System would be a highly effective tool in training her company's sales force. But she also did it because she personally wanted to lead the effort. "It was absolutely cutting edge in terms of learning and design," she explains. "I had a passion for it, I wanted to work with it. The best way to do this was to get my company to become a client. And then to get them to put me in charge of rolling it out!"

Persuading her company to acquire the technology, at a cost of more than one million dollars, required all Julie's persuasive powers. This brings us to the next step in creating your own work. You must devise a practical plan for persuading your organization to adopt your suggestion.

Doing this requires that you:

- Gather and verify your data
- Decide exactly how to present your idea
- Discern who you need to talk to
- Anticipate objections
- Set forth the reasons why you should head the effort

Julie followed these steps. She became an expert on the new system, undergoing many hours of training. She learned all she could about competitive systems in the market. She recognized the need to sell her company's CEO and his team on her idea. And she figured out a succinct and powerful way of advocating for the project. "My line was: it's all about speed and access. We can train our salesforce twenty-five people at a time. Or we can put six people on airplanes and fly them all over the world to do the training, keeping them on the road for months. *Or* we can roll out the training in Singapore, São Paulo and Des Moines all on the same day. We can get this training into the company's water system all at once."

Julie understood that it was necessary to match what she wanted to do in the company with the organization's mission. She says, "At the time, the company was focusing on just-in-time delivery for our products—getting stuff out to customers as soon as they needed it. We were also trying to devise new channels we could use for fast delivery. So I emphasized that the ASK System provided a way for us to deliver just-in-time *training* to our people, giving them access to new skills when they were needed. So absolutely using the System worked with our mission. And that's why I was able to make it work for me."

Integrate your passions

Julie Anixter talks about the role that passion has played in her history of creating satisfying work. Many of us over the past few years have begun to speak of our work in a similar way. We'll say, "This project gets my juices flowing," or "I'm going to do this job in a way that knocks everyone's socks off." We'll even say, "I feel that this is what I was born to do."

Yet talking like this is a fairly new phenomenon. You used to hear it only from visionary entrepreneurs and people in the arts. The industrial economy honored rigid divisions between people's work and their passions, and also limited the satisfaction of decision-making to a small group. Thus it was assumed that most individuals worked only to make money to live on, and indulged their interests in their private hours.

And so the accountant pursued her passion for sailing on weekends. The retail manager practiced her love of cooking whenever she had the chance, piling recipe books by her bedside for nighttime reading. The Italophile lawyer spent every vacation traveling in his favorite country, and took Italian-language classes one night a week. The grocery distributor who adored gardening spent time between clients sketching out new designs for plantings and poring over seed catalogs for new finds.

Passions were thus categorized as *hobbies,* which distinguished them from "real" work. People spent money on hobbies, rather than earning money in their pursuit. When one applied for a job, no reference was made to hobbies. They were considered irrelevant to the workplace, their purpose being to occupy leisure hours.

As I mentioned in Chapter 1, the U.S. Congress in 1965 proposed a cabinet-level Office on Hobbies to help people cope with the oceans of leisure time that a computer-dominated workplace was expected to unleash. The very fact that the congressional report envisioned hobbies as *the antithesis of work* reveals the prevailing mind-set. If a cameraman took up fly-fishing, there was no notion that he or she might find a way to make a living from it.

But integrating our passions into our work is something that more and more of us are seeking to do. And this integration is an essential aspect of creating our own work.

I'm thinking of a newswriter for a local television station. He was respected in his work but had come to see it as basically just that—work. He was a man with wide interests, who felt increasingly frustrated because his writing job seemed removed from the many things he cared for, and he was starting to feel burned out as a result. One day, his division decided it needed to focus more on leisure activities, and he proposed doing a short piece about learning to fly, one of his many hobbies. He persuaded his boss to let him produce it. The brief segment reflected his own distinctive voice, which is quirky and humorous, and it proved an immediate success. So he began proposing other brief pieces, all based on his interests. Now he moves between producing and writing with ease, and takes far greater satisfaction in his job.

When we find ways to manifest our passions in our work, we create something that is unique to us as individuals. In essence, we claim our work as our own.

And so the accountant who loves sailing begins tailoring her practice and pursues sailboat manufacturers and professional racers for her clients.

The retail manager who adores cooking persuades the store she works for to sponsor cooking classes and wine tastings in Europe. She arranges and leads these ventures, which in turn enable the store to recapture the upscale business it had previously been losing.

The lawyer who is mad for all things Italian becomes a specialist in intellectual property rights around the globe. She goes on to represent a publishing conglomerate based in Milan, and ends up doing half her business in Italy.

The grocery distributor begins selling his specialized produce at a local farmer's market, discovers a demand for certain hard-to-locate herbs and vegetables, and turns his beloved garden into a thriving business.

Over the past ten years, we have grown accustomed to such stories. They appeal to our imagination. We see them as tales of individual triumph. But too often we dismiss these tales as having any relevance for us. We tell ourselves that the people who achieved these successes must have been unusually creative or entrepreneurial. We dismiss them as evidence that some people have all the luck.

And so we may continue to feel stuck, bound by a kind of mental paralysis that keeps us from integrating our passions with our work. And the fact that so many others seem to be doing just that only makes us feel worse.

The first step out of this bind is to recognize that bringing our interests to bear upon our work has become easier with every passing year. And to understand that the same forces that make life in VUCA such a challenge also present us with great opportunities to adapt our work to suit our individual passions. Being able to do this is not the result of being lucky, but rather of being able to read our environment with accuracy and skill. Then we can figure out where our particular opportunity might lie.

There are three ways that the world of work has changed

to allow more scope for our passions. These include the emphasis on the niche, better access to markets, and easier access to capital.

1. *The emphasis on the niche.* The knowledge economy thrives upon identifying and serving ever-smaller and more specific niches, rather than addressing the huge mass markets of the industrial era. This creates opportunities for us to develop and market limited quantities of customized goods and services, rather than the mass production runs that used to dominate. And because products and services are so specialized, they can be combined and offered in highly individual ways.

This means that if you are a benefits manager whose great love is teaching, you can develop a course for human resources executives in your specialty and market it through a satellite-based adult-learning company, setting up a partnership between that company and your own.

It also means that if you are crazy about wood strawberries, you can develop a broadly faceted yet highly targeted business based on finding, planting, identifying, propagating, lobbying for, distributing, and creating recipes for your beloved berry.

2. *Better access to markets.* The Internet makes it possible for us all to access large, even global, markets directly, speedily, and with little expense—and to take advantage of established online networks rather than having to build our own.

This means that if you are a public relations specialist who happens to love croquet, you can exchange information about players and tournaments across a wide network, develop an electronic newsletter based upon this exchange, and distribute it to fellow aficionados around the world. You can then market yourself as the world's best-connected croquet fan, and bring in new business for your firm based on that.

And it means that if you're a massage therapist whose child has a muscular disorder, you can learn about physical therapy techniques that are of particular help to your child, then communicate with other parents whose children share the disorder and help connect them to appropriate services, developing a specialty as you extend your knowledge and connections.

3. *Easier access to capital.* In the industrial era, starting almost any kind of enterprise required a substantial capital investment. Unless you were rich, a bank was the only means of securing the money. This meant that you either had to have a personal relationship with a banker, a stellar track record, or hefty collateral.

This is no longer true. Venture funds of every size exist to provide support for people with good ideas. Groups ranging from the Social Venture Network to the New Venture Lab stage the equivalent of open casting calls, inviting individuals to submit proposals that might be of interest to investors. And individuals finance new ventures using credit cards.

Just as significant, many large companies have units whose purpose is to identify and fund new ventures in related fields, or finance internal "skunkworks" efforts that are exploring potentially fruitful new markets and ideas. Intel, for example, now funds more start-ups that are the result of someone's passion and vision than any venture fund in Silicon Valley, many of them founded by former Intel employees.

Other organizations help employees get grants to develop worthwhile ideas, or provide other kinds of financing. A nurse-practitioner at a Boston hospital recently devised a bandage for a patient with a complicated but common kind of wound; the hospital then sponsored her application for a patent on it, and helped her set up a unit to manufacture and distribute her invention.

The ways of reconciling our passions with our opportunities are as diverse as we are. The keys to doing so are imagination and determination. Both are exemplified by Katherine Armstrong, formerly one of the brightest stars at Johnson & Johnson, an executive in her early thirties with an M.B.A. from the London School of Economics whom the company was grooming to be a visible and influential corporate leader.

Katherine joined J&J after graduate school. She says, "I had never considered myself a corporate type. I ended up getting an M.B.A. because I needed something to do when my husband took a job with Citibank in London just after we were married. My field of study was ethics, not corporate finance. But I did some work for J&J in school and saw what a good company it was. So when I was offered a job at corporate headquarters, my husband and I decided to move to New Jersey. Without really thinking about it, I was in the corporate system."

Katherine enjoyed considerable success at J&J, and she was put on the fast track, given major assignments in different operating companies. During this time, she had two daughters in two years. She says, "We were living a very demanding lifestyle, in the corporate suburbs of New Jersey, where there's all this emphasis on keeping up. I didn't feel that I shared a lot of the values of people I was around, but I was living in a very similar way. I was consumed by work. I loved my job, and I loved my family, but I was beginning to hate my life. I didn't see how I could have the kind of family-centered existence I wanted and still be a corporate executive. I know a lot of women do it, but it just wasn't me."

Something had to give, and after long and searching talks with her husband, Katherine resigned her job. "We decided we needed a more low-key life in a more low-key place." She moved with her family, the girls then aged two and four, from suburban New Jersey to rural New Hampshire. Her husband also left his job as a commodities trader and began to work for a number of clients online. Katherine started consulting for J&J on a five-day-a-month contract, writing speeches and developing themes for the company's social responsibility initiative. She also devised a program of health fairs aimed at women employees.

This focus reflected Katherine's original interests, as expressed in graduate school. It also enabled her to spend much more time with her family. But she still felt the need to knit her work more closely with her dreams. Just before she resigned her job, she and her husband had visited the camp he had attended in the summers as a child. "During that visit," she says, "I was struck by two recognitions. First, the lifelong attachment Rob had to the place. Second, the positive mentor-buddy relationship that the college-aged counselors had with the children. I've never seen young adults thrive so much in leadership positions, or children connect to authority in such a productive and emotional manner. At the same time, I saw young children of the staff running around and having a great time. Altogether, it felt so wholesome, so grounded."

After they moved to New Hampshire, Katherine's husband began to talk about his desire to own and run such a camp. He began attending American Camping Association conferences, and Katherine joined him. "Through the workshops and conversations, I began to see how my talents, experiences, and values could contribute to what had previously been his dream alone. I realized it was something we could do together that would let us enjoy the kind of family life we wanted."

Katherine and her husband began looking for suitable property on a New Hampshire lake. Acquiring and running a camp such as they envisioned would be expensive, and Katherine recognized that having a guaranteed clientele would help her and her husband to secure adequate funding. That's when Katherine thought of Johnson & Johnson. Why not offer employees of the company a chance to send their children to the same camp every summer? What could be a better way to build community within the company? What could be more helpful in terms of retaining employees? And what would work more seamlessly with Katherine and Rob's plans?

The longer she considered it, the better the idea seemed. Employees could use the facilities during the year for retreats. Like the summer camp, the retreats would reflect Katherine's interest in yoga and nutrition—appropriate for a company that manufactures health products, employs large numbers of medical professionals, and sells to doctors and nurses as well as the consumer market. If J&J were interested, the company might want to partner in funding the enterprise.

As Katherine became convinced the idea had merit, she and her husband set about doing the groundwork, assessing their skills, making new connections, and gathering information. As she got more deeply involved with the camping association, she ended up creating a workshop for its members on creating a values-based culture. To do so, she drew from her work for J&J. She also took a part-time position as a residence adviser in a dorm at a nearby college, in order to get counseling experience.

She says, "The camp is a very long-term goal. We need to find the right piece of land before we get our funding and partners in place. And we need things to come together in a way that works. It's tricky, so we're not putting a time frame around it. We're taking it slow, and learning as we go. We're developing the skills and connections we need to do something really extraordinary. Meanwhile, we've found a way of living that better reflects our values. And we're heading in a direction where our family life and how we earn our living will all be part of the same thing. Not compartmentalized, as they are in the corporate world."

Not all of us are in the position to work out comfortable consulting arrangements like Katherine Armstrong. But many of us can find better ways to integrate our responsibilities at work and at home, which is indeed another way of integrating our passions with our work. For example, Amy Rottinghaus, a young associate at Ernst & Young in Cleveland, felt increasing dissatisfaction because she and her husband (also with Ernst &

Young) spent weeks at a time on consulting jobs in different cities.

Amy explains, "We had just gotten married, and we were basically seeing each other only on weekends. It didn't seem like a very good way to start!" The problem lay in the fact that the company treated each of them as a separate employee, whereas they were trying to create a life together. So Amy and her husband began examining their assignments, looking for overlap: clients for whom they might both work, but on different jobs; cities with several clients where each might be posted at the same time.

They then devised a business plan showing specific opportunities that they could fill in a way that would allow for a more balanced married life. They itemized the potential savings to the company if they were able to work in the same city. They then prepared a plan to present to their bosses, anticipating objections and pointing out advantages. Other colleagues heard what they were doing and began to ask about it, which sparked new ways for other employees to think about resolving similar problems. Eventually, Amy's husband decided to enter graduate school, which kept him in Cleveland, but their attempt to find a creative solution influenced the company nonetheless.

Efforts like Amy's, made by individuals acting one at a time but seeking to address a common problem, point the way to fresh approaches for us all. Taken together, these efforts are sparking a revolution. Ric Giardina, an Intel employee whom I interviewed for a previous book, noted how change took place in his organization. He said, "The process of change is not like an inkstain. It's not something that starts in just one place and then spreads all around. It's more like a lot of little individual splatters that keep getting bigger and bigger. And then some of them start to come together and coalesce."

Just so. Individualized solutions to general dilemmas are *precisely* what organizations need right now. Most companies recognize this. Their great concern is attracting and retaining talented people, and they understand that the issue of balancing work and life is a problem. But they can't rely on their human resources departments to come up with all the answers, because one size no longer fits us all. And so *we* need to start contributing answers. Each one of us needs to seize the initiative and find ways to help our organizations discover how to make the most of our talents.

We have to teach our organizations how to work with us if we want to bring the full force of our enthusiasm and passion to our work.

Identify your market

Whether you create your own work in partnership with an organization, within an organization, or entirely on your own, doing so requires that you identify your market, devise strategies for reaching it, and decide how best to represent yourself to it.

Connecting directly with your market distinguishes it as your own. Connecting directly with your market also adds to your value. And connecting directly with your market expands the parameters of your web (see Chapter 6, Strategy Four), giving continuity to your passage through life.

Thinking in terms of markets—rather than bosses, chains

of command, lines of report, or tasks that must be completed—is an essential aspect of creating your own work. For in essence, creating your work involves a shift from doing work that has been assigned to selling work that you design and believe has value. And you can't sell successfully unless you:

- Know who you are selling to
- Understand their needs
- Recognize the intersection between those needs and what you have to offer
- Communicate that point of intersection powerfully and persuasively

By assuming responsibility for what you put out into the world, and then advocating for it and representing it, you make your work fully *yours*.

This is why creating your own work puts you in the same position as an artist, a musician, or a writer. Making paintings, playing music, and writing stories is only part of an artist's work. Creating an audience that can appreciate it is the other part. Not *finding* an audience, but *creating* an audience, for every influential piece of work builds a community, a constituency, a market, where none existed. Every influential piece of work addresses a need or interest that went unarticulated and unrecognized until it was produced.

No one was interested in fine art whose subject was commercial products until Andy Warhol created an interest in it.

No one expected traditional jazz to have a major resurgence until Wynton Marsalis made it happen.

No one believed there was a need for a personal computer

until Apple built one and persuaded people that they not only needed one but could use it as an instrument of personal liberation.

Andy Warhol, Wynton Marsalis, and the Steve Jobs/Steve Wozniak team at Apple created extraordinary, vital, pathbreaking products—silk screens of American icons, great music that reinvigorated a classic tradition, personal computers that are versatile and user-friendly. What these artists created reflected their individual talents, aesthetics, and interests. But what they created *also* built a market that supported and sustained their work.

Andy Warhol did it by persuading people to reconsider the relationship between commercial and fine art, and to abandon the idea that an object has to be unique to have value

Wynton Marsalis did it by returning jazz to its roots, reinterpreting the music for a younger audience in a way that captured the romance, professionalism, and swing of the great big-band ensembles, as opposed to the self-absorbed atonal complexities that had dominated the music since the late 1960s.

The two Steves at Apple did it by understanding that the social revolution unleashed in the 1960s had in turn made people more skeptical of large organizations and less willing to depend upon them. They knew that offering people control over the technology they used to do their work would have the long-term effect of giving them greater control over work itself, and that people wanted this control and were ready to assume it.

Apple is indeed as perfect an example of creating a market as has been seen in this century. The team at Apple wasn't building a product to satisfy the demands of corporate technology directors, as IBM had done when marketing its main-frames. They were building a product for *a market that did not yet exist.*

When the Apple II was introduced in the early 1970s, it was widely assumed that only the most dedicated hobbyists would want to buy or use one. As an IBM executive declared at the time, "There is simply no market for a personal computer." But Apple *built* a market by stirring the interest of an unusual coalition: students, technology buffs, social and community activists, graphic designers, and self-publishing entrepreneurs.

Apple's slogan at the time reflects its founders' understanding that identifying and forming a market is as important as creating the product or service itself. Their slogan was simply *"Real artists ship."*

Real artists ship means that real artists have markets. If you want to create your own work, you have to assume the attitude of an artist *and* you have to ship.

In addition to identifying your market, you also have to manage it. How you do this is determined by how you structure your work.

If you work in partnership with an organization, your primary markets will be internal to that company—those inside who buy or use your services and their bosses. If you work alone, you must build your markets in the external world.

Handling each of these calls for different approaches, different skills.

Katherine Armstrong skillfully created her own work in

partnership with Johnson & Johnson, not just in regard to her long-term goal of starting a summer camp but also in her role as a consultant. She says, "With J&J, I have a partnership. I get to create my work, pursuing my interests as they intersect with those of the company. What I like best is the thought and conceptual work I do: researching, distilling and reflecting on how the whole issue of social responsibility plays out at J&J. I'm basically in a position where I can identify projects that I think we should be doing, and then pull together a team to do them. And I can do this because I have identified who my *internal* markets are."

For most of her projects, Katherine's internal markets are the corporate VPs for public affairs and communications, to whom she reports; the corporate officers whose interests she represents and whose mission her efforts are aimed at supporting; the many decentralized operating companies that make up J&J; and those companies' customers and outside partners. Reconciling and articulating the interests of each of these markets with one another is a fundamental aspect of what Katherine does.

She describes how this works for the series of health fairs she has designed for J&J's women employees. "With this kind of project," she says, "the operating units are obviously my market, since it's where the employees are, and they're the ones whose needs I'm trying to serve. But human resources is also my market, because the fairs are a means of motivating employees, which serves retention, and retaining people is a primary mission in HR these days. Also, HR is where I'm going to get most of the budget for the project. So they're my partner in this as well as my market."

In a more subtle way, J&J's corporate parent is also Katherine's market, because her project is designed to support their mission. "At corporate, the great aim now is to find ways of pulling together the various parts of the company *not* by sectors, like cosmetics and eye care, but by markets or technologies. The goal is to take a much more integrated approach. So any activity that breaks down the sectoral divisions serves the corporate interest. The women's health fairs do that, because they cut across sectors and make their appeal based on a market—the market, in this case, being women. So we have consumer products like Neutrogena alongside biotech research units whose work is aimed at improving women's health."

"For every project," Katherine notes, "I need to consider which of all the various entities in the company might be markets for what I am doing. That means I need to understand all of their different missions, address their various concerns, and include them all in the effort. I also need to make use of their various staff in the teams I pull together, so that my projects will have buy-in in the units." And so the real art in managing internal markets, according to Katherine, lies in "figuring out how to reconcile the various interests of your different markets, so that you can do your project in a coordinated way."

Achieving this often requires creating new lines of communication that cut across the organization in surprising ways so that the interests of each market can mesh with that of the others. As Katherine notes, "This is one of the most important and difficult things I have to do. At J&J, the operating units tend to see corporate as a bunch of bean counters, while headquarters has a hard time keeping in touch with the base. My projects cut across barriers, so I have to find ways to encourage people to communicate across lines. That means creating channels that allow them to do so. This is where having a great network inside the company comes in. You can't create new channels of communication without that."

Having a broad network within an organization is thus an essential aspect of creating work in partnership with it. So is having connections at the senior level. As Katherine points out, "Being able to go directly to senior executives gives you two things: credibility throughout the rest of the company, and access to funding. If you don't have those, you'll waste a lot of time doing proposals that just sit on somebody's desk."

Katherine's experience suggests a blueprint for creating a partnership *within* an organization:

- Identify each of your internal markets
- Determine the interests, mission, and concerns of each
- Understand how they mesh with or contradict one another
- Represent the interests of each market to one another
- Create new channels of communication between the different markets
- Make creative use of staff people from your different markets
- Cultivate senior people who can support you

When you create your work on your own, your internal market is essentially yourself. When you start out, your external market is likely to be entirely undefined. Your primary job is to define and develop it, then to keep it growing and to manage it.

Jim Rosenberg faced this task when he began to consider how he might set himself up as a humor writer without leaving his hometown of Greensboro, North Carolina. Like many of the people interviewed for this book, Jim had begun his career with a false start. He had become a lawyer.

"So why did I become a lawyer?" he asks. "It's not like I had any real interest in the law, or even knew what a lawyer did on a day-to-day basis. It was more the result of what I think of as the smart student syndrome. You get good grades, so you go to college. You do well in college, so you get an M.B.A. or go to law school. It's like it's what you're *supposed* to do, like the world has a set of outcomes, and all you have to do is get into the stream. Once you're in it, you end up in this big container pond that might not have anything to do with *you*. I was smart, so I became a lawyer. I didn't really think about what I was doing. But once I got a job as a lawyer, I found out I hated it. I was with a good firm, and I earned good money. But I knew right away it wasn't for me."

After a few years, Jim left his law career to join a small company run by his father; the idea was to gain time so he could explore what he wanted to do. "I helped to make my dad's business profitable, which was my goal. But I knew I was just coasting. I made it bearable by doing stuff on the side. I wrote a humor column for the local newspaper, and I had a quiz bowl game show on local TV. These things kept me going, although they made hardly any money."

Jim's true love was for humor. "If I'd started out twenty years ago, it probably would have just been a hobby. There aren't many opportunities for humorists with a family to support in Greensboro. Especially since my main interest was developing original material." But today the situation is different, and, using the Internet, Jim has developed a market for his work.

"On the Internet," he says, "there's space for the little guy. And you get to *create* your space, you don't just fill it. It used to be that, when people were hunting for a job, they were looking for a place to park themselves—a place someone else had left open, a place they could occupy. Those days are *over!* On the Internet, there's no more parking lot, no ready-made space you can just slip into. Now you define your space."

Jim was intrigued by the extent to which e-mail had become a vehicle for sharing humor. "We hardly even think about it, but it's incredible the extent to which the Internet has become a medium for circulating jokes. It's been like that from the start. Realizing this made me understand that people are hungry for humor. There's obviously a market for it, and technology makes it possible to reach any market you want. So the questions I had to ask myself are: How do I find that market? What's the best way to reach it? And how do I figure out a way to make it pay?"

Jim began by sampling the market. "I went to all the humor sites I could find. I analyzed what they all did. I immediately saw that the most important thing you need is a personality, an identity, on the Internet. It's such a personal medium, very one-on-one, which means you have to define yourself very clearly. You have to do something that sets you apart. At first, I was just writing humor items and submitting them to sites, as if being funny by itself was enough. But as I became familiar with the market, I realized that I needed more continuity. You can't just be funny. What you put out there has to hang together. It has to contribute to your *identity.*"

So Jim decided to concentrate on doing monologues. "After all," he explains, "It's their monologues that made Leno and Letterman rich and famous, not their interviews. So I became Mr. Monologue—that's the online identity I created for myself. It's both my identity and my specific form. When I want to comment on something, it comes from the desk of Mr. Monologue. My wife is Mrs. Monologue, and the kids are the little Monologues. The family is definitely part of it, they're all characters that my subscribers know."

Jim began posting his monologues on other humorists' websites. He says, "I quickly learned that a lot of people in the online humor community share their sites, publishing other writers' material in a way that enables those other writers to get known. That's how the online world works: there are whole portions of the Internet where great stuff just gets given away. *That's* the key to building new markets. The people who understand the medium recognize this, and are amazingly generous with their space. But of course, it comes back in the end. They feature you, then you feature them back, and that gives everyone more exposure. Plus people come to them because they want to link to you, and vice versa. I think this generosity is built into the technology of hyperlinks, because hyperlinks work most powerfully when you facilitate a lot of points of connection."

Once Jim had excited some interest, he set up the Mr. Monologue website, learning as he did from his efforts. He says, "A lot of people make the mistake of trying to get as many links connecting to their site as possible. But I learned by doing it that that's the wrong approach. What you *really* want is links to the four or five biggest sites in your area. I've also realized that websites are not the best vehicle for what I'm doing. We've all just come to accept that a website is the way to create a business online. But in a lot of ways, e-mail is better. e-mail is really the Internet's killer application. It's what people *use,* it's why people sign on with a service provider. So I started building a list of subscribers to the Mr. Monologue e-mails. The list went from zero to twenty thousand in almost no time, because I had gotten so much material published on other peoples' sites. I'd used those sites to build an identity and a following in the humor community, which is huge."

Once Jim's list reached twenty thousand, he had enough strength to begin finding advertisers to sponsor his e-mails. "I didn't even have to solicit, people approached me once my name was out there. For now, that's the easiest way to get paid, with sponsorships and ads. In the future, there'll be some simple way to charge small amounts—twenty cents or so—each time someone on your subscriber list opens one of your e-mails. The technology's not there to do that in a quick and cheap way just now."

Jim points out that an Internet identity brings in other paid work as well. "Because I'm Mr. Monologue, people come to me to give speeches, write articles, and do freelance projects. So creating an online identity is also a way of building more business, as well as being a business in itself."

Jim's relationship with his market involves a lot of give-and-take; he gets ideas from his subscribers that he then works into his material. This both expands his subscriber base and strengthens his ties to it. His close involvement with the market he has created is characteristic of how Internet enterprises have operated almost from the start. Those who regularly use such sites, or subscribe to e-mail services, expect those sites and services to reflect their ideas and respond to them as individuals. They feel the services they use are in some sense "theirs," part of their self-definition—which is why self-definition is so important for small players, the self-described "little guys" like Mr. Monologue.

This is also why web-based enterprises tend to relate to their markets like radio stations, which regular listeners often consider integral to their identity: news junkie, hard-rock freak, classical music devotee, jazz fan, country lover. In this way, radio is different from network television, a medium in which viewers relate to specific shows rather than to channels (although the newer networks such as Fox are trying to change this) and where personalities tend to be fairly generic as a result. As with the radio, the eagerness on the part of customers and clients to identify with the web-based products and services they use is a characteristic, and a strength, of the niche approach.

The lesson here is that if you are trying to create a strong niche using support from the Internet, you must *develop, refine,* and find ways to *represent* your individual personality. For it is above all your individual identity that will tie you to your external market. Your clients and customers will seek you out because they relate to what you offer. And your offers must be clear and reflect who you are. That's one of the lessons in creating work on your own that Mr. Monologue teaches. Other lessons include:

- Respond in a highly personal way to those you serve
- Seek to keep strengthening bonds with customers and clients
- Give some of your work away
- Share space with others in your field rather than considering them competitors
- Integrate all the parts of your life into your persona
- Create, rather than seek to fill, your space

Run your own shop

Barbara Roberts, the CEO of Acoustiguide, the company that customizes museum tours (we met her in Chapter 3), believes that creating satisfying work for yourself depends upon two conditions. "First, you have to love what you do and feel passionate about it. Most people know that. But second, you also have to know what kind of environment you feel comfortable in and find ways to create it. You have to know *how* you like to do your work, what processes are right for you. This is just as important as loving what you do."

Barbara says that, in her experience, people are much quicker to find out *what* they want to do than they are at identifying *how* they want to do it. "Most people know what their interests and passions are, but a lot of them haven't articulated, even to themselves, the kind of environment they want to be in. And they tend to be more willing to compromise on their environment, even though it's a major element in what they live with every day.

Barbara gives an example. "I left Wall Street *not* because

the work didn't engage me, but because I hated the culture. I couldn't stand the way people there worked with and related to one another. I know lots of people from my time there who are just as miserable as I was, but they've stayed on for twenty years. Somewhere along the way, they decided that their workplace environment just wasn't all that important. But you can't feel in control of your life unless the *way* you work is congenial to you."

Barbara is right. Shaping an environment that enables you to work in a way that is compatible with your style and needs is both one of the imperatives—and one of the rewards—of creating your own work. Whether you work within an organization, in partnership with an organization, or on your own, your ability to structure your time and complete your tasks in a way that reflects your personal style is an essential aspect of your freedom, your creativity, your satisfaction. In addition, *how* you do your work is as much a part of your signature, as much a part of what distinguishes you and gives you value in the market, as what you actually produce. And structuring your work to fit your particular needs is yet another step toward the increasing integration of work and life that characterizes today's postindustrial frontier.

In structuring your work to reflect your needs, it is helpful to think in terms of *running your shop.*

What is your shop? And how does your shop differ from your office? Drawing a distinction between the two can be helpful.

An office is *a place,* but a shop is *a place where things get done.*

An office implies a unit in a bureaucracy, whereas a shop implies a nexus of commerce presided over by an individual.

The concept of the shop has a double meaning. It can be a retail outlet, a space in which sales are made and goods transferred. Or it can be a workshop where things are fabricated—physical items, but also ideas.

Over the last hundred and fifty years, as our world became increasingly industrialized, the importance of the shop waned. Items were more likely to be assembled, rather than fabricated by individuals, and marketed through increasingly impersonal outlets.

But as we move away from an industrial economy toward ever-smaller niche markets, the notion of the shop begins to reassume importance, both as a place of development and a space for sales. A premium is placed on items that are handcrafted, that bear the mark of a workshop. And intellectual property—information, ideas, knowledge—is the lifeblood of our economy.

And so, whatever you do—whether you are an Internet humorist, a copy editor, a real estate agent, a sales rep, an accountant, a human resources executive, a nurse, a software programmer, or a hairdresser—you can benefit by thinking of your business as your shop. And you can benefit by considering carefully how you want your shop to run. Your shop is an extension of *you,* and the more it reflects your values and your personality, the more exciting, rewarding, and niche-specific it will be.

When you run your own shop, you define yourself as independent. Your shop is a manifestation of your confidence and commitment. Your shop is yours, even if you work for someone else. Your shop can be your cubicle, *but it is also your way of operating in the world.* It is defined by its processes as well as by its physical space.

I first became aware of the importance of the shop when I was researching an earlier book about women's ways of leadership. The women leaders I studied each had highly distinctive styles, and their styles were manifest in how they worked, in how the people around them were encouraged to work with one another, and in the physical layout of their workplaces.

Dorothy Brunson, who at that time owned and operated a chain of radio stations based in Baltimore, made a particularly vivid impression. She had two side-by-side offices, each for doing a different kind of work. Each office was built entirely of glass, so as not to cut her off from her people, and both were in the very center of her larger office suite so that everyone who came through had access to her. Outside her door was an old, beat-up kitchen table that served as an informal gathering place, a hangout, for her staff. The table really served as a kind of hearth around which her entire operation revolved. Dorothy's shop thus reflected the highly familial, personal, informal, and unconventional style of her personality, which was manifest in both the physical space and in how things were done.

What does it take to run your own shop?

Just as you need to start at the core to identify your passions, so also do you need to start at the core to give shape to your shop. How you like to work is intensely personal. Your true workstyle comes out when you have a major deadline and need to focus. Where do you go? What do you do?

How you like to work often relates to early experiences of times when you felt especially comfortable, perhaps working alongside your parents in the kitchen, the garden, or the basement workshop. Or it might recall memories of doing a project with a group at school.

To figure out what shape your shop should take, you need to reconnect with some of these memories. Using Erin Thomas's timeline or Chris Cappy's self-assessment tool in Chapter 3 can be helpful.

You also need to ask yourself some questions:

- When do you like to get up?
- Do you like to go straight to work, or do you prefer to take your time?
- What period of the day is your most productive?
- Do you like low-level noise while you work, or do you find it distracting?
- Do people coming in and out stimulate or irritate you?
- Do you like to do several things at once, or one thing at a time?
- Are you formal with people or informal?
- Do you prefer a rapid or a relaxed pace?
- Do you like to be always busy, or do you need a lot of downtime?
- Do you prefer group gatherings, or meeting one-on-one?
- Do you move around during the day, or stick to your desk?
- Do phone calls break your concentration or bring you fresh ideas?
- Do you like to cluster your e-mails, or answer them as they come?

- Does a messy desk distract you, or make you feel as if you're getting something done?
- Do you have to clean your desk at the end of every day?
- Are regular meals important to you, or do you snack when hungry?
- Do you have a strong need to get outdoors during the day?
- Do you become depressed or sleepy when deprived of natural light?
- Do you love meeting new people, or prefer to stick with people you know?
- Do you value a lot of discussion, or does it make you impatient?
- Are you interested in learning new things on the computer, or dismayed by the very thought of having to do so?
- What tools do you use in your daily work?
- What tools do you most enjoy using—in any kind of work?
- Are you more productive when you concentrate on doing a single thing in a day, or when you spread your energies to address a variety of issues?
- Do you derive satisfaction from performing a wide range of tasks, or do you prefer to delegate much of your work?
- Do you need to ruminate before setting to work, or do you like to plunge right in?
- Does your mood swing back and forth during the day, or is your energy steady?
- What do you fear most: change, or being stuck in a rut?

Each of these questions needs to be considered when you are thinking about how to run your shop. Of course, there are no right or wrong answers. Your answers are simply tools for helping you clarify and understand your particular style. To run your shop effectively, you need to address your own comfort and understand when you are most productive. But you *also* have to give those around you scope to create a comfortable way of operating for themselves. You want your shop to be lively and open to new ideas. If you impose your own style too rigidly, you will inhibit those around you.

Running your shop so that it's comfortable for you is in many ways easiest if you work on your own, since you don't have to accommodate other imperatives. But it takes discipline, a good deal of self-knowledge, and the ability to motivate yourself every day. Loneliness and isolation are constant threats, and can lead you into the temptation of spending too much time with friends over lunch or on the telephone, just to satisfy your need to stay in touch.

Creating work on your own is thus probably not a good idea if your answers to the above questions indicate you thrive on the stimulation of constant interaction. Procrastination is also easier when no one is looking over your shoulder, so if this is a problem for you, working alone may not be wise. Many people who succeed at working alone set themselves fairly rigid schedules. They answer e-mail only at the start and the end of each day and don't take personal calls before six. They dress professionally even if they're in a bedroom office.

Adopting these kinds of habits is a way of reminding yourself of where you are. You are in your shop.

Working in partnership *with* an organization affords a lot of leeway in terms of designing your environment, yet gives you a ready-made set of colleagues and associates with whom to interact. Sunny Ralfini creates fund-raising events for Nordoff-Robbins, a British nonprofit that sponsors music programs for children with disabilities. She works *with,* rather than *for,* the company. She finds her own office space, sets her own budget, raises the money she needs to cover it, decides upon what kinds of events to sponsor and whom to invite.

Sunny says, "One of the best parts of my job is that I have the freedom to design how I work. I am very deliberate about it. I don't have the freedom to choose my office—we operate from donated space—but I do get to decide how I want to use it. I've made the decision to have no staff, something I could easily have if I raised the money to pay for it. I *do* hire people temporarily to help with specific projects, especially those that require a lot of data entry and big mailings, but generally I do just about everything myself. For one thing, I like having a lot of variety and doing a lot of things during the course of any day. And I like being directly in touch with our sponsors and partners."

Sunny also prefers not having a staff because she finds it is more efficient. She says, "I often find myself working with people—sponsors, the musicians who contribute their performances, their agents and recording companies—who have these enormous staffs, which is absolutely typical in the music business. If I schedule a meeting with them, they usually arrive with all these people in tow, ready to take notes, make points, and do a lot of delegation. So we have what I call crowd meetings, where there's a lot of talking and everything takes a really long time, and the participants get to feel as if something is really happening. But I know that the main purpose of the meeting is really just to make people feel as if they are part of the effort, part of the team. The real work will get done afterward, mostly on the phone."

Sunny's style has evolved as a result of her personality but also reflects her experiences, what she has learned during many years of working. For example, her distaste for cumbersome meetings comes from exposure to another kind of business. "For years, I worked in office space donated by the Hard Rock Cafe," she says. "I had my shop right there in their corporate offices. Well, in the restaurant business, time is money, so you don't squander it in meetings. The staff had one quick meeting first thing in the morning, and that was *it*."

Now her office space is donated by a large record company, and things are entirely different. "Like most corporate settings, this one is overstaffed, so everyone's a bit afraid of being dispensable. One way people deal with this is to keep incredibly busy with constant meetings, and it becomes hard to avoid being constantly roped in." Running her own shop, Sunny enjoys the benefits of controlling most of her time. "Naturally, I participate in some of the meetings, but I kind of put them in a frame. And because I don't have a staff, I'm not adding to the glut. I really value efficiency, see it as part of what I have to contribute. If I had to spend a lot of time preparing for meetings so that I could impress the right people, I wouldn't be able to accomplish all that I do."

Setting your own hours is only one aspect of running your

own shop. Representing your values in the world is just as important. Simple things such as returning letters and calls give evidence of your style and your personality, and make clear where your priorities lie. Erica Gruen, a former advertising and cable executive who, among other things, was the founding CEO of the Food Network, is presently working in partnership with a number of technology and cable start-ups as a consultant and investor, and manifesting her values is part of how she runs her shop.

Erica says, "I think I've always had a very distinct way of operating, but now that I work with partners instead of within just one company, I can be even more explicit about how I like to do things. Basic matters such as politeness have always been important to me—returning phone calls and e-mails immediately, for example. I do it, and I expect it. That's a big part of my style. Also, one thing I've always enjoyed is connecting people with one another; I find it a huge source of gratification. I don't take fees for doing it, but it's part of what I do, part of what I offer."

Within an organization, running your shop can be a bit trickier, but it is no less important, especially if you want to establish yourself as an independent contributor with strong values who brings a lot to the company. In the industrial economy, only bosses got to run their own shop, setting the tone for the whole organization. Their ability to do this distinguished them from the rest of the cogs, all of whom had to go along with someone else's program.

This has begun to change as organizations flatten, teams become more flexible, work is addressed on a project basis. And it is changing as individuals with desirable skills come to understand their own individual power and challenge the traditional ways of doing things. Something as seemingly insignificant as "casual Fridays" is an indication of this cultural swing.

Your company may be comfortable letting you run your shop, setting the policies and practices that define your work. Or it may be uncomfortable with even the prospect of such a thing. It may be stuck in the old hierarchical mind-set, assuming that only those at the top get to set the rules.

If this is so, your task is to help your organization make the transition to a way of operating that is more appropriate for today's VUCA environment. Your task is to articulate your needs and to explain why having them met is important, in terms of your productivity and your ability to innovate. Your task is to help your organization change in ways that will make your own life better and benefit the company as well. If the task is impossible, you need to take inventory of your skills and begin to look around.

Target multiple centers of gravity

The imperative, and the opportunity, to create our own work presents us with a number of paradoxes. If we create our work from our passion, this implies that we are passionate about our work, which in turn implies that we are fiercely devoted to the path we have chosen.

But life in VUCA is characterized by rapid and unforeseen changes that can come from multiple directions. This in turn requires us to be flexible, to adjust our expectations as conditions alter.

In such an environment, it is dangerous for us to *count* on anything working out. And it is dangerous to anticipate that a successful venture will remain so over time. Yet if we are *not* strongly committed to what we venture, it will be difficult for us to summon the strength and creativity required to make the innovations we attempt a success.

How do we manage these contradictions?

We spread our risk.

We spin off multiple variations of our projects. We anticipate making adjustments. We target multiple centers of gravity. We become well versed in the concept of polyvalency, in which a variety of options balance and harmonize with one another.

Kevin Kelly, editor-at-large for *Wired* magazine, who earlier noted that every new technology both creates and supplies new needs, also observes that the whole concept of what constitutes "a career" is changing. In the past, a career was about mastering a specific set of skills so that we could perform a predefined series of functions and by doing so progress along a predetermined path. But today, careers increasingly resemble what Kelly calls "networks of multiple and simultaneous commitments with a constant churn between new skills and outmoded roles."

Bill Taylor, publisher of *Fast Company,* says the same thing in simpler language. He notes that, "Being flexible in today's environment is absolutely essential. That's why I think in the future we'll see someone working thirty percent of her time for a company like Xerox, thirty percent of her time for some small venture in which she is invested, and thirty percent of her time on some totally unrelated project that she really cares about and that adds to her set of skills. How all these things blend together will reflect what we want out of life. And what we want will be the glue that holds everything together." Creating our own work, then, in Taylor's definition, is about *piecing together a variety of opportunities.* The nature of our passion is reflected in how they are combined, in the distinct pattern they make, as much as in their substance.

Erica Gruen, the former Food Network CEO who is now working as a consultant, agrees with this assessment. She says, "I've come to think about a career like I think about a stock portfolio. It needs to be balanced. It can't be too weighted in one area, you can't put all your eggs in one basket. This means that *all* of us have to learn how to keep a couple of balls in the air. We have to devote ourselves to what we're doing, but we need to roll it out in a couple of different ways or it won't be balanced."

Balanced passion. It's a paradoxical concept, but it's one we must understand and practice if we are to tame the new world of work. As with running our own shop, what ties together our various efforts is *how* we do things, as much as the various things we choose to do. How we manifest our values and how we do things gives coherence to our efforts, identifying them in the marketplace as uniquely ours.

6

Strategy Four:
Weave a Strong Web
of Inclusion

Our individual security today lies more and more in our networks—in their size, their variety, their breadth, their depth, and their strength. Our value as individuals is vested in the web of connections we are able to build up over the course of our lives. We thrive in proportion to their power.

Even a generation ago, having a strong network was far less crucial than it has become today. People then could afford to be socially low-key, even withdrawn, if that was their choice. They could afford to keep their relationships separate and distinct—neighbors in one sphere, colleagues in another—making little effort to bring them together or forge links among them. Your parents and the neighborhood in which you grew up may have been like that; I know mine certainly were. When I was growing up, only charismatic extroverts, small-business owners dependent upon community contacts, and vote-eager politicians seemed to feel the need of having a broad and far-reaching personal circle.

Things have changed. Why?

First, things have changed because we can no longer rely

upon organizations to take care of us throughout the course of our lives. The only real security we have today is that we can provide for ourselves. And broad connections are an essential aspect of that security. They provide us with an infrastructure of support.

Second, things have changed because our economy is built on networks, and it is the law of networks that they are powerful in proportion to their size. Nothing in today's economy can stand alone. Even the most established organization is no longer a self-contained enterprise but rather a web of interconnecting alliances, partnerships, affiliations, and relationships. Our way of operating as individuals thus needs to be in sync with the networked environment that shapes our work.

The growth of the Internet over the last five years has only strengthened the emphasis upon relationships. HTML, the language of the World Wide Web, is built on linking and therefore requires those who use it to think in terms of links. One characteristic of a strong network is that *it creates links among others,* strengthening all who are a part of it. And so in building our infrastructure of support, we must strive not only to link ourselves with others but to create links among those within our web. In addition to being a technology that *requires* us to build strong webs, the Internet is also a tool that *enables* us to do so, providing the means for us to stay in touch with a broad range of people—quickly, easily, and cheaply.

And so the true end of the industrial age might be said to have occurred when the notion of "networking" as an important business and personal skill came into general use. This oc-

curred in the early 1980s. Those were also, of course, the years
when the importance and stability of large organizations began
to decline, depriving people of the ready-made—though highly
restricted—webs to which they had formerly almost automatically belonged.

I prefer to think in terms of "webs of inclusion" rather than
networks when describing how we as individuals build our
systems of support. The word *network* has a distinctly mid-
eighties ring, conjuring up visions of the shallow and mean-
ingless exchange of business cards between people who will
never see one another again. Used in this way, the term implies a certain level of impersonality, distance, and calcula-
tion. At its worst, it suggests the tendency of "networkers" to
use other people rather than bring them together.

A web of inclusion, by contrast, implies an organic image
and describes the primary means by which powerful networks
operate—that is, *by inclusion*. I first used the term in *The Female Advantage* to describe the structure I found in organizations run by some of America's best women leaders; in a later
book, *The Web of Inclusion,* I studied how webs can work in organizations without regard to gender.

How is a web of inclusion different from a 1980s-style
network?

*A web of inclusion operates across boundaries and divi-
sions, and thus becomes a powerful force for breaking them
down.* When you build a web, *everyone* gets included, from
your aunt in Ohio to your former boss to the mechanic who

fixes your car. The people with whom you reconnected at your last high-school reunion are a part of your web, as is that headhunter you encountered at a professional conference last fall. They are part of your extended circle, in which the personal and the professional are both represented. By contrast, a network tends to be exclusively professional.

A web of inclusion requires continual maintenance. It's not simply a question of gathering a lot of business cards and entering the names in the e-mail directory of your electronic organizer. That's creating a database, and having a well-organized one is necessary to building a web, but it does not constitute a web in itself. Building a web requires that you keep in touch— not with everybody all the time, but on a fairly regular basis with a large cross-section of the people in your web. It requires that you reach out, that you ask for help when you need it, that you give help when you're asked and when you can. It requires that you respond to requests quickly, even if it is only in order to graciously answer in the negative. How you use your mail defines how you do your business. Thus, a web of inclusion suggests a way of operating in the world, as well as being in itself a structure.

A web of inclusion flourishes when you connect the elements within it, weaving and strengthening the fabric as a whole. You are at the center of your web, and everyone you draw into it is connected to you and through you. Your work is both to strengthen the ties that bind those in your web to you *and* to create ties between and among those in your web. To the extent that you do so, your web will serve those who are part of it as well as yourself. For a powerful web is not simply a structure of relationships. *It is a generator of relationships as well.*

Building a strong, broad, and sustaining web is not only practical in today's environment. It is also extremely rewarding. As we strengthen and expand our support systems, we test ourselves in relationship with many different kinds of people. We become both more self-reliant *and* more trusting. We enrich our lives now while preparing ourselves for the uncertainties of the future.

Some people are born websters. They seem to know everyone, to have the gift of meeting people wherever they go. They get on a plane in New Orleans and get off it in Denver having made two new lifelong friends. They have someone to look up, whether they're in Los Angeles, Madrid, or Moscow. They turn up at dinner parties in towns they've never visited before.

But what if you're not one of them?

What if building a web doesn't play to your own particular strengths? What if you would rather immerse yourself in a book on a plane than chat with whoever happens to be occupying the next seat? Isn't there some contradiction between the strategy that says Start at the Core—that is, *know yourself*—and this strategy, Keep Building Your Web of Inclusion?

To some extent there is, *but that is no reason for not building a web.* For doing so skillfully does not oblige you to change your basic nature. Instead, it requires that you make the effort to acquire some basic skills and use some basic techniques that anyone can master.

These include:

- ❖ Join or start a professional group
- ❖ Go deep fast
- ❖ Understand the strength of weak ties

❖ Grab the spotlight
❖ Look people up
❖ Do web work every day
❖ Enter into the economy of the gift

Join or start a professional group

Targeting a group that you want to be part of is key to building your web of inclusion. Your web will consist of personal friends, people you went to school with, relatives, former teachers, people from your neighborhood and community, parents of your children's friends. It will also include a broad range of professional colleagues. To expand this last group takes some effort. You need to move beyond just the people you meet at work. You do this by being part of a professional network, and absorbing that network into your broader web.

A professional network can be formal or informal. It is simply a group that connects you with people who share your workplace interests or expertise. It's a means of expanding the pool of people you know while also contributing to them. Still, as anyone who has done so knows, simply joining a professional group is never enough. It can be difficult to penetrate the inner sanctum (especially when the group is a large one) if you do not have the right means of entrée, do not know the inside people, or have not been a member for a long time. If you join a ready-made network, you need to become active within it, to find ways to put yourself at its center. Ways to do so will be discussed later in this chapter.

A more powerful approach can be to *start* a network of

your own, for if you do so, you will automatically be at its center. This will make it easier for you to both connect with others and to forge links among the people whom you know. A powerful example of this kind of self-created network is one begun by Marshall Goldsmith, a well-known executive coach and consultant. Five years ago, Marshall attended a Renaissance Weekend at Hilton Head after Christmas—one of those invitation-only retreats famously attended by the Clintons when they were in the White House. The gathering inspired Marshall to put something similar together for a group of friends and colleagues.

Marshall says, "I love participating in the Renaissance weekend—I do it every year. It's a great way to meet people and be stimulated by new kinds of thinking. Still, it's a very big group, and that works against getting to know other participants very well. Plus the atmosphere can get pretty competitive, since people come from all kinds of fields and the main thing they have in common is being very successful. My idea was to create a kind of mini–Renaissance weekend for my friends, people I figured might have a lot in common. Basically, I wanted to introduce them. I wanted to bring some people I knew together. The idea was, here's a chance to meet some people you'll probably like and to see if we can do some good in the world. And if business opportunities come out of it, that's great too."

Thus was The Learning Network born. The Learning Network is a group of about fifty people in Marshall's field—coaches, consultants, and writers who study leadership and organizations. Most work on their own, moving from project to project, and as a result often find it hard to establish ongoing links with colleagues. The centerpiece of TLN is a three-day gathering in Del Mar, California, on the second weekend of every January. At these gatherings, participants share what they have been been doing over the past year, talk about what they want to do, and discuss what projects they might do together. It's an extremely casual gathering, with lots of small-group sessions and plenty of open space. The evenings are usually spent at Marshall's nearby house.

The yearly sessions have changed over the five years of TLN's existence. During the first two gatherings, the group focused on ambitious schemes for what they might do to improve the world. But over the years, it became more focused on what members could do to help one another—although the group as a whole has contributed to a number of books, money from the sales of which is donated to nonprofit organizations.

The most noticeable development, however, has been an increasing emphasis on people's personal lives. Several members' illnesses, one death, and the death of several spouses have played a role in emphasizing the personal rather than the professional relationships between the members. In addition, many members have formed deep and sustaining friendships with others in the group, and this has made the ties closer and more personal. As a result, The Learning Network has evolved over the course of its five-year life into an unusually powerful infrastructure of support.

Several decisions have resulted in the group's harmony and closeness. For one thing, the size of the group has remained stable. Every member has several people whom he or she would like to invite in, and the criteria for belonging (basically, being a friend of Marshall's) has come to seem more arbitrary as time goes on. Still, the group now has a history and a shared dynamic, and is wary of expanding, lest its intimate and personal character be lost. However, spouses of original members who work in the same field have been invited to join the group, which lends a familial feeling to the gatherings.

Despite the personal emphasis, business opportunities have developed, especially for the coaches who are members of the group. And Marshall's latest brainstorm has been including TLN's members in a new venture he has undertaken in partnership with the *Financial Times,* providing organizations access to a wide range of thought leaders by using an interactive video-conferencing system. Inclusion in the partnership increases everyone's visibility and multiplies group members' connections in the wider world.

TLN very definitely bears Marshall's stamp. His personal motto is "Life Is Good," and this finds an echo in everything the group does. Yet because it has remained small, cohesive, and stable over time, the group has also been shaped by the individuals who constitute it. Marshall is at the center of the web, but the tendrils of connection between various members have grown stronger through the years, and these individual relationships create new patterns of connection. Fellow members are meeting one another's friends and colleagues from other circles, which extends everybody's reach and draws members into new and ever-expanding webs.

It took a lot of organizing on Marshall's part to put TLN together. He called everyone, invited them, reserved a block of rooms at a Del Mar hotel, and put together a tentative agenda of events—small groups alternating with large sessions in which members brainstormed on specific issues. Everyone invited paid his or her own expenses, and for the first few years Marshall assumed the expense of the conference room and meals, which today is assumed by members. Marshall facilitated the first meeting, but that job too now rotates among members. "This is the fun part," says Marshall. "Now I just get to be a member."

What turned the disparate individuals who attend the gatherings into a true web were the follow-up efforts that Marshall originally made. Everyone submitted an informal biography, and these were printed up into a book. This was distributed along with everyone's contact information. In the first year, members received a lot of e-mail from Marshall's office informing them of what other members were doing and creating a context in which various members could keep in touch.

By the end of the second gathering, relationships began to develop. As various members had ideas for projects—business ideas or ways to earn money for nonprofits—they began to contact one another directly, often notifying other members when they traveled to their city. Since many traveled frequently, some began e-mailing their travel schedules to other members. As a result of these efforts, Marshall doesn't need to put in all the effort he did at the start. Group members don't need a conduit or an organizer any longer. TLN has developed a strength and resilience of its own. Marshall remains at the heart of the web, the individual who has defined its culture. But the web has developed its own logic, shape, and characteristics, its own way of being.

Go deep fast

Karen Van Dyke, the event marketer whom we met in Chapter 3 asking her dreams for guidance, is an expert webster. Her ability to put herself at the center proved especially helpful when she was uprooted to Orlando, where she had no connections beyond her husband. Karen knew that, as an independent contractor, she had to create a web fast. She went about it with her typical gusto.

One of the first things she learned upon moving was that *Fast Company* magazine was preparing to host a conference at a Disney facility in Orlando. The magazine's conferences are typically coordinated and in part staffed by members of *Fast Company* "cells," which are groups of the magazine's fans who meet regularly to discuss ideas and trends. Karen had been a member of one such cell in California. Now, in Orlando, she volunteered to help coordinate and market the upcoming conference.

Karen says, "The cells are a great way to connect with people who share your interests. They're not really networks in the old sense of everybody trying to promote themselves and get business in a purposeful way. The cells are more about ideas, a way for people to come together and learn from each other. You need to be able to do that in a time when everything is moving very fast, and you need a lot of information to figure things out." Karen notes that although *Fast Company* sends packets to group coordinators to use in putting the cells together, there are no criteria for belonging, no structure beyond monthly meetings. "Basically, you just walk in and say 'Hi, I'm so and so and I'd like to help.' That's all it takes to become a member."

When Karen arrived in Orlando, the local cell had been dormant because of the coordinator's travel schedule. So Karen immediately took steps to revive it. "I got a list from the magazine of all the people in the area who had attended their conferences in the past, and a list of sponsors. Then I got in touch with them all. I let them know that I was reviving the cell and reinstituting monthly meetings. I persuaded people to come and I chaired the meetings. I set up discussion topics, and coordinated things with the magazine. Since I didn't have my own business really going yet, I had lots of time to do this. I figure that by the time my business takes off, someone else will be ready to take over." Here she echoes Marshall Goldsmith: "Then I can just be an ordinary member of the group."

Karen emphasizes that discussions at the cell meeting integrate personal and professional concerns while also fulfilling intellectual and emotional needs. "We talk about real issues— how the world is changing and how we can navigate it better. And how people think things are going to change in the future. Because everything is moving so quickly these days, we are all really *creating* the future. Being part of a cell gives you clarity about that, and helps you to see that we are all really making things up as we go along."

For this reason, building a cell requires different skills than the old 1980s networking did. Above all, says Karen, it requires that you be able to *go deep* with people. She says, "I think being able to go deep with people very, very fast is the absolute key to creating a strong web today, because the things we are dealing with are very hard and very important."

What does *going deep fast* mean?

"It means connecting with people at a fairly profound level

in a short amount of time," says Karen. "It means moving past the chitchat, past the exchange of titles, past where you went to school and who you know, so you can get directly to the important questions. It means asking people right off the bat: What's your big issue just now? What's hard about what you're trying to do? What do you find easy? What led you to your present path? Where are you hoping it leads you? What helps you? What doesn't help? What do you *need?*"

Karen believes that such questions can be asked quickly if you do it in a sensitive way. She says, "Somehow, people know I'm not digging, I'm not prying, I'm not trying to get something on them or invade their space. I'm searching for knowledge about the person I'm talking to. I'm searching for stuff I can relate to, for common ground, for whatever I can learn. Most people are really open to this thoughtful kind of inquiry about what they're going through. When people don't respond, you know they don't have much interest in going deep."

Karen notes that going deep with someone "doesn't mean that person becomes your best friend for life. Not at all! You may never even see him or her again. It's just a way of jump-starting the process of connection and making sure that your conversation has real meaning. What makes going deep fast possible is *intuition.* I don't think you can go deep quickly unless you have worked on your intuitive powers, unless you listen to yourself at a gut level. Somewhere inside, you *know* what kinds of questions you need to ask, what will bring the other person out, what will lead to a fruitful and intimate conversation, what is appropriate. Going deep quickly is really about using intuition to discover common ground, so you can bring someone into your web. By doing that, you'll learn things and you'll probably be able to help the person you connect with. And in the process, you'll probably get more clarity about what *you're* trying to do."

Understand the strength of weak ties

Researchers who have studied people with broad and deep webs have observed that such people understand what they call the "strength of weak ties"—friendly acquaintanceships that can be warm and intense, and may last for decades, but that don't necessarily lead to close friendships. People who are *not* skilled at building wide-ranging associations tend instead to shy away from close and searching conversations with anyone whom they sense might not become a close friend. This is in part because they fear that the relationship could become invasive, and feel they wouldn't know how to handle it should that happen. And it is in part because they tend to consider mere acquaintanceships to be shallow and pointless.

As a result, people who are poor web-builders either make an effort to avoid new relationships altogether by behaving in a standoffish way or exhaust themselves trying to turn every acquaintance into a close friend.

Sociologist Mark Granovetter examined the usefulness of weak ties in his landmark book *Getting a Job,* published in 1974. He interviewed hundreds of professional and technical workers in a Boston suburb and found that nearly 60 percent had gotten their jobs through personal connections: by knowing people in the community, at previous jobs, or from school.

The big surprise in his study was that only about 16 percent of these people reported that they often saw the contact who helped them find the job; the rest reported seeing that contact either occasionally or rarely. That is, people tended to get their jobs because of *the broad circle of their acquaintance,* rather than through people to whom they were close. What mattered in terms of finding a job was having an extended web. Thus Granovetter argued that, in terms of negotiating the world of work, having a lot of weak ties is profoundly important.

Writer Malcolm Gladwell quotes Granovetter's study in a *New Yorker* article that examines the phenomenon of people who seem to "know everyone." They are, he concludes, basically people who understand the "power of relationships that are not close at all." For his article, Gladwell uses as his lens a woman in her seventies who is neither rich, nor beautiful, nor special in any obvious way, a woman who in fact can seem shy and somewhat eccentric. Her name is Lois Weisberg.

Weisberg is presently Chicago's commissioner of cultural affairs, but she's had a lot of jobs throughout her life. She is also the kind of person who "knows everyone," the kind of individual who always seems to be at the center of a multiplicity of webs. She is the go-to person in Chicago if you want to get anything done, if you're new in town and want to meet people, or if you're trying to find a job. She is what Gladwell calls a "connector," someone whose power comes from the sheer size of her web of acquaintances *and* her ability—her indefatigable eagerness—to connect the people within it to one another.

As Gladwell notes, there is a Lois Weisberg in every city, someone who is at the center of many different webs and who serves as a major point of intersection. Someone who is not shy about inserting himself or herself into new groups and drawing other people in as well, thus creating a tissue of interconnections. Karen Van Dyke, putting herself immediately into the center of the *Fast Company* cell in Orlando, is on her way to becoming one of these people in her region.

Gladwell notes that it is because of "connectors" that things in communities get done. New groups are established, nonprofits are staffed, jobs are found, projects undertaken, alliances formed. We don't all have to become like Lois Weisberg—many of us would be exhausted by the effort. But we can learn valuable lessons from Gladwell's study of people like her.

What do people like Lois Weisberg do?

They move in and through a variety of circles.

Gladwell observes that one reason the Lois Weisbergs of the world are effective is that they know a lot of people from a lot of different circles. For example, Lois has held a wide variety of jobs. She started a drama troupe. She worked for an underground newspaper years ago. She did public relations for an injury-rehabilitation institute and later for a public-interest law firm. She was a director of special events for the city, coordinating flea markets all over town. Because of the range of her employment, and because she has always been a community and neighborhood activist, she knows people from among the following groups: politicians, park lovers, writers, actors, visual artists, lawyers, architects, people in the hotel business, newspaper columnists, and local publicists, as well as a vast network of flea market aficionados.

Gladwell says that the most powerful "connectors" are

people like this, people who move among different circles.
They serve as the point of connection among very different
webs, a means for bringing people into one another's orbit.
Thus, they always seem to be at the center of things.

They keep up ties over a long period of time.

Gladwell observes that people move in and through Weisberg's web *but never really move out of it.* Many of us have
held a variety of jobs or joined different groups over the years
but have fallen out of touch with the people we knew as a result. Not Lois. She keeps in touch—not constantly, but unself-
consciously when she feels it is important.

For example, she doesn't think twice about phoning someone she met many years before if she needs their help, thinks
they might have something to contribute to a project she is engaged in, or has an idea she believes might be of use to them.
The words "he probably wouldn't remember me" are simply
not a part of her vocabulary. To really leverage the strength of
weak ties, this attitude—that of course someone will remember you and be pleased to hear from you—is necessary. It is
also necessary to keep an updated Rolodex, and have the wits
to track down people who have been out of your orbit for a
while.

They reach out to others first.

Weisberg is a master of approaching people she has never
met before, people outside her circle, people with whom she
does not, on the surface, have all that much in common. Gladwell offers an example. Lois was driving through Chicago one
afternoon when she noticed a young woman trying to prevent a
group of park workers from carting a beautiful sculpture away
from a rundown park. Lois jumped out of the car to see what was

going on and began talking to the young woman, asking her questions to discover the source of her concern—or *going deep fast,* to use Karen Van Dyke's phrase. Then Lois got two newspaper writers to interview the young woman and write a story on the fracas. Next, Lois introduced her new friend to other people interested in restoring and maintaining Chicago's parks. Within a year of meeting Lois, the young woman had become president of the board of a group called Friends of the Park.

They connect people they don't know all that well.

The woman protesting the statue's removal was a young mother new to the neighborhood. In addition to sending out newspaper reporters to interview her, Lois called another woman she knew slightly, who had a child about the same age and lived on a nearby street. The two younger women soon became the closest of friends because Weisberg was not hesitant to introduce two people she hardly knew.

Here we can learn another lesson. Many of us are reluctant to connect people unless we know them very well. We worry about being presumptuous, about the people we bring together not liking one another. We worry about getting caught in the middle. Lois, on the contrary, is casual about connecting people and does it constantly, trusting they will decide for themselves if the relationship is worth pursuing. She is forever on the lookout for what people might have in common—a situation, proximity, interests, experiences, friends.

Taking a few lessons from Lois Weisberg can be an enormous help in learning to master an environment in which change is constant and we must always be attentive to what we might be doing next. For if we can provide ourselves with the basic infrastructure of a strong and sustaining web, we are far more likely to know about new opportunities coming up. A strong and broad web, at its most basic level, provides us with a lot of information.

But a strong web's value is greater than that, for the new world of work requires us to constantly market ourselves. And the most powerful kind of marketing has always employed that most mysterious, unquantifiable, and yet irresistible force, word of mouth. Advertisers and publicists spend hundreds of millions each year trying to spark word-of-mouth interest: in a Hollywood movie, a new kind of shoe, a just-published novel, a television series, a magazine, a car, a brand of sports equipment, a breed of dog. Despite the intentionality, the phenomenon of word of mouth remains serendipitous.

Malcolm Gladwell believes he knows what makes it work. He believes that people with Lois Weisberg's skills have the "power to spark a word-of-mouth contagion"—a contagion that in fact follows the pattern of an epidemic, spreading out exponentially in a series of waves from a tiny epicenter, spiking out along the tendrils of a web. Because people like Lois have huge, diverse, and ever-expanding webs, they can spread new ideas and new information with extraordinary rapidity. And because they serve as the point of connection between entirely unrelated webs and so knit together varied and isolated segments of society, they are pivotal enough to be able to compel others to take notice. *This* is the ultimate power of the true connector, the power to spread ideas and information. And in a fast-changing and volatile world, being one of the people who can do so is an invaluable skill.

Grab the spotlight

By leaping from her car to wade into the center of the statue controversy, Lois Weisberg made herself instantly visible. Of course, her behavior is not for everyone. But there are many kinds of equivalent actions, and each one of us needs to find ways to compel attention that are comfortable for us. The truth is that simply joining a group will do very little to build and strengthen our web if most members of the group have little idea of who we are. Having weak ties does not mean we should be invisible to large numbers of people. Rather, those with whom we have weak ties always feel that in some sense they *know* us.

Erica Gruen, the former CEO of the Food Network, whom we met in Chapter 5, told us that one of her great joys in life is connecting other people. She's a woman with a strong and active web, which she has fashioned through meticulous attention and maintenance. She created that web by making herself as visible as possible.

Erica is in many ways an anomaly. She is an unassuming and neighborly friend-next-door midwesterner who achieved notable success in the tough New York world of television and Internet start-ups. She is also someone who "doesn't care at all about things, about clothes, about having a new car or a fabulous apartment. I think you become powerful when you have financial security, and the way to do that is by being frugal. That's what gives you freedom. Feeling I am secure and having a great network: that's what has been responsible for my success."

Like Lois Weisberg, Erica has held many types of jobs. She started out as a psychologist, managed a music program for a college, became an arts administrator, then an advertising executive. She says, "I have never really planned my transitions, but I'm always on the lookout for what might come next. And the one thing I've really been diligent about is looking for opportunities to put myself forward. If I'm going to a conference, I volunteer to be on a panel. I try to give as many speeches as I can. If you go to a conference and you're just another person there, you can stand around all night with a drink in your hand and talk to no one. But if you're on a panel, you've got a ready-made group of people to interact with. Plus people in the audience will come up and talk to you. That's how you get to know people: by making yourself visible whenever you can."

Erica also understands the power of the media to make her more visible. She says, "No matter what my job, I've always made it a priority to try to find ways to get quoted in the media. I've made myself a spokesperson in whatever job I had, and worked to cultivate reporters in the trade and national press. And I was always quick to return their calls. I hang around with reporters so that I can get a good idea of what they want in a story, what kind of statements grab their interest. To me, that's all part of making yourself visible. So is writing—seizing any opportunity to write a piece that relates to what I'm doing in my work. If I'm part of a professional group, I always contribute pieces to their newsletter. And I'm constantly working on my presentation skills, especially writing and speaking."

.   .   .

How did an unassuming person like Erica become so canny about making herself visible? She is very clear about her motives. She says, "When I was first in advertising, I had a very powerful mentor. She taught me an enormous amount, and she also protected me from the political cross-currents in the company, although I didn't realize that at the time. She died quite suddenly, and losing her was terrible—she had meant a lot to me. But even in the midst of my grieving, I began to recognize how vulnerable I was without her. I had *no* visibility in the organization. Without her, I had no power."

Erica realized then that she had to become more of a presence, both in her organization and in her industry, since she was unsure that she would be able to hold onto her job once a new boss was named. "So I did something that was totally out of character for me, really *bold*." A lot of the agency's clients were in the cable television industry, which was fairly new at the time and really wide open. Erica had received a letter from a professional group made up mostly of presidents of cable networks. The group ran awards programs and did a lot of promotional work for the industry. "The letter was just an ordinary press release," Erica recalls. "It was the kind of thing I wouldn't ordinarily have paid much attention to, but I was really looking for a way to make new connections. So I called a woman who was part of the group, whom I knew very slightly. I said I'd noticed that no one from the advertising community was represented in the group, and wouldn't it be in their interests if I joined it? I really took a flyer on that one, but she agreed it was a good idea."

Once she was part of the group, Erica decided to try for a position on the board to extend her visibility and her connections. "Because I wasn't a cable television president, it was unlikely that I would be put on the board, but I knew that was the best way to get to know people. So I worked at it, calling people and inviting them to lunch, finding out what their concerns were, really campaigning. Once I got elected, I was at the center of what was happening in the industry."

Erica's boldness and tenacity were soon rewarded, for a few months after her election to the board, her new boss did indeed let her go. But through the connections she had forged in the cable industry, she was invited by one of her fellow board members to assume the leadership of one of his new divisions. That's how she came to head up the Food Network.

We can all learn from Erica's efforts to make herself more visible in a way that was comfortable for her.

First, she exhibited both boldness and imagination by suggesting herself for membership in a group of cable television executives that had never included anyone from the advertising business before.

Next, she drew on the strength of weak ties by calling a woman she knew only slightly to propose herself for membership, and she framed the idea in a way that reflected the group's interests.

Then, she immediately sought to strengthen her position in the new group by assuming a pivotal role, rather than expecting to broaden her web simply by joining.

Finally, she worked hard to get to know the board members personally, thus broadening and strengthening her contacts, which proved useful when the time came for a new job search.

Look people up

People who are great web-builders look people up. If they are going to be in Seattle, they call someone they have met who lives there—someone they might not even know very well—and ask if there is anything going on that they should know about. Chances are that the person they have called will either offer to meet them for lunch or dinner, or invite them to a gathering where they can meet a whole new circle. If a web-builder doesn't know anyone in Seattle, he or she asks colleagues or friends if there is anyone they should get to know in Seattle.

As Erica Gruen says, "Once you take an active role in building your web, you begin to see how it all works. People with whom you actually have very little connection will go out of their way to help you, while people you've known forever often don't." With this observation, Erica echoes what sociologist Granovetter learned in his study about the importance of weak ties. Erica extends the idea by adding, "People who *aren't* good at building webs tend to see the same group of people over and over—friends from school, people whose social set they want to be part of, those in their immediate circle at work. But this is incredibly limiting and not all that useful when you need help. Also, it's not all that interesting!"

Having a broad range of connections, says Erica, is "basically just a question of being open, of making yourself available, and of having something to offer. My attitude is, I always want to meet new people—I never know what might come of it. Of course, a lot of times the connection doesn't come to much. But you can always refer that person on, connect him or her to someone else."

Looking people up is a habit, but a few essentials make it easier to do. The first prerequisite is having a well-organized database. Looking people up often seems like too much of a chore if you first have to spend time digging up someone's number, or if you have to rack your brain's trying to remember the name of that guy you had such a great talk with at your association conference last year in New York.

One of the drawbacks of e-mail is that most address books are arranged so that they list only people's names and e-mail addresses. It's not unusual to have a regular e-mail correspondence with someone but have no idea where they live. If you want to look people up, you need a computer database that allows you to keep all the coordinates for large numbers of people, including the details of precisely where they live. That way, you can click on "Seattle" when you're about to make a trip to that city and find contact information for everyone you know there. In addition, you need to maintain your database on a regular basis, adding new people as you meet them and updating information.

Great networkers also keep other kinds of information in their databases. In writing about Lois Weisberg, Malcolm Gladwell also examines the practices of Roger Horchow, founder of Horchow's catalog and another person who seems to "know everybody." Horchow keeps personal information on people in his database: their birthdays, their likes and dislikes. This enables him, when for example he tries out a new Chinese restaurant that he thinks is great, to send a quick message about it to everyone he knows who loves Chinese food. It's a way of keeping in touch, a way of saying *I'm thinking about you.* As Erica Gruen observes, the line between being a great web-builder and being an exceptionally thoughtful person is indistinct. "Building a web is about knowing people and finding ways to be of service to them."

Do web work every day

Maintaining an extensive and updated database sounds like a lot of work. In our 24/7 world, who has the time? But it's a question of having your priorities straight, of focusing on what is important rather than what is urgent, of creating opportunities for the future rather than responding to the crises of the present moment.

In Chapter 3, we looked at the importance of doing a daily assessment. I wrote about how, in assessing how I spent my own time, I began to realize that I was always in the habit of taking an all-or-nothing approach to my activities. I either wrote all day, burying myself entirely in my work, or spent a lot of time socializing with friends. I either took a bike ride and went to the health club and walked forty blocks, or I got little exercise beyond stepping around to the corner deli. Charting my own patterns, I resolved to introduce greater balance into my life by pursuing a greater variety of activities every day. To that end, I made a list on the last page of my daily notebook of all the areas of my life that were important to me, and resolved to do *one thing* each day that addressed each area of importance.

One of the categories on my list was "Connecting with people." By this, I did not mean spending time with family and friends—the people I am close to were put in a category of their own. Rather, I meant attending to and extending my web of inclusion. Most of the work of doing so is easy and takes only minutes of my time: responding promptly to e-mails and calls, putting people in touch with one another, sending brief greetings to people I haven't spoken with in a while, thinking up ways I can help other people with their projects, entering new names and addresses into my database.

These are the kinds of chores that are easily put off, and I had put them off in the past. And because the work involved rarely seems urgent, it often never got done. However, I found that putting in a little time on "webwork" every day gives me a different perspective. Rather than regarding the unexpected phone call from a reader who has a question as distraction from my "real" work, I am now able to regard it as an essential part of what I do, part of the fabric of a normal and productive day. Rather than fret because entering a few new addresses takes up time when I "should" be doing something else, I now understand that this is in fact what I *should* be doing.

The key, of course, is not to get bogged down, not to spend a disproportionate time answering that unexpected query, not to feel guilty if you're called on for help and can't fill the request. If there's nothing you can do, you can always refer people on, as Erica Gruen does. That's not passing the buck—it's extending and broadening the circle.

Enter into the economy of the gift

Jim Rosenberg—Mr. Monologue—got his start building a substantial list for his e-mail service by posting humor items *on other humorists' sites.* Jim says, "There are two things necessary for creating an identity on the web. The first is to have a persona, an identifiable personality, a niche. The second is to enter into this strange economy of the gift, where you benefit by being more concerned with what you can give than what you can get."

Jim notes that his greatest boost came from Cathie Walker, of Victoria, British Columbia, who has one of the most popular humor sites on the Internet. "Cathie got where she got by viewing everyone as a potential collaborator, rather than as competition. She went out of her way to promote anyone she thought was good. She'd post your stuff, let you link through her. Of course, that put her at the center of the humor community—*she* has become the link, the center."

The Internet forces us all to confront the need to *give things away*. This is because information and content on the web are notoriously hard to copyright, because everything can be copied quickly and cheaply, because everything can be forwarded to someone else. Esther Dyson, the technology guru, believes that the Internet will make the whole idea of intellectual property obsolete. "You can't hold onto it," she says, "there's no way you can retain it. So you need to use it to spread your name around and create the demand for yourself in other venues." For example, Dyson believes that in the future it will be impossible for authors to make money from their books. Their books will just be a means of sharing their ideas with the world. And, by bringing attention to those ideas, those books will create a market for their authors—to moderate panels, lead chat rooms, give speeches, and make personal appearances. And these opportunities, according to Dyson, will be the source of authors' income in the next economy.

Giving things away is the quickest way to build a web. That's how companies such as America Online achieved dominance. At the start, they simply offered their service for free. People signed up with AOL because it cost nothing *and* because their friends had signed up for the same reason; this was important, since in the early days it was far easier to connect with people who had the same service provider. It wasn't until AOL became the dominant player that the company began charging $21.95 a month.

AOL's value lies *not* in the superiority of its technology but in the breadth and depth of its user web. And AOL built this web by aggressively giving its service away. Those who accepted the offer, those millions of points of connection, *created the company's value.* Without them, without its web, AOL would be nothing.

Cathie Walker, who helped Jim Rosenberg get started as a humor writer, exemplifies how the lessons of AOL can be applied on an individual level. She built her business entirely by using the principles of the inclusive web, operating from a position of generosity. She's a prime example of how powerful this strategy can be in an economy based on networks.

In the mid-1990s, Cathie was an assistant administrator at the University of British Columbia, on the island of Victoria. She liked her job well enough, but she preferred fooling around on her computer and especially enjoyed browsing the humor sites. She loved the sense of escape they provided and enjoyed sharing the amusing content she found with people at work.

Above all, she liked the sense of community on the Internet, which was still quite small at the time. Cathie says, "There weren't many personal websites then, but I was intrigued with those I saw. I thought, you know, I could do that. So I bought myself a book, *Teach Yourself HTML in Seven Days,* and began to use it to build a site."

Cathie's site was basically a series of bookmarks, a directory of her favorite humor sites. She stuck a picture of Mr. Potato Head on it as her mascot and called her site The Center for the Easily Amused, which has since been changed to amused.com. She says, "Since most sites in those days were academic, mine was immediately refreshing. It was kind of the online equivalent of taking a comic book into the bathroom at work, to get a couple minutes of stolen time to yourself and have a laugh or two." She e-mailed everyone who had humor sites and introduced herself. She asked if she could link to their site as a way of promoting their work.

From the outset, she figured her site would be popular, because she knew from a lot of online surfing that the most successful sites were those that let the personality of their owners shine through. "And I was very much the voice behind my site, the editor. I put my own taste out there. It was *me.* I was like the host of *The Gong Show,* choosing the contestants."

The site was Cathie's hobby; she worked on it before she went to work and after she came home at night. Then Netscape picked up her site and listed it under its "What's New" advisory, which brought so much traffic that it caused her service provider to crash. With the huge increase in visitors, Cathie was able to start selling ads through an online agency, which earned her a few hundred dollars a month.

At this point, she realized that she needed to start providing original content on her site. "I was getting this reputation as a really silly place to be, and people were logging on. I needed to become more than just a directory. Well, it should have been a problem, because I couldn't write code, I had no time and I had no money. But I *did* have this online community that was very strong, and I had worked hard to develop personal relationships with people who were part of it."

This is where Cathie's generosity paid off. She says, "People in the community knew that I was a collaborator. They knew that I had always worked to promote their work. So *they* provided me with what I needed. People would send me content—jokes and cartoons. One guy redesigned half my website at no charge. Another guy translated content into code. In return, they knew that I would try to draw as much attention to them as possible. Since I got a lot of traffic, it all worked out very well. People like Jim Rosenberg were able to develop a following. Basically, *my role was sharing my list* and helping people to use it to their advantage."

After a few years, Cathie's site was bought by an Internet company and she was hired to manage it. She still runs her site in a highly personal manner, choosing all the material and getting involved in online discussions. Having created her own work, Cathie was able to leave her job for one that came from her inner core. Her only resource has been the network she has built through her frank admiration for, and generous promotion of, the online humor community. She says, "I basically went to people and said, How can I help you? What can I do to promote your work? I wasn't preoccupied with what I could get, but with what I could *give*. And that's what made the whole thing work."

. . .

Carlos Marin, the San Diego consultant we met in Chapter 3 compiling his family history, echoes what Cathie Walker says about the role of generosity in this economy, but he puts it in the context of building a web of support. Carlos says, "Everyone these days needs to consider where his or her support will come from, because the old supports, the old sources of stability, are *gone.* And the most powerful way to start building that support is to ask yourself not what you need, but *what you have to give.* You can't build an effective support system if you're preoccupied by what you will *get.*"

Why is this true? Carlos believes that it is partly because it's hard to *know* precisely what you're going to need in a time when everything is changing and partly because you have no way of knowing who will end up giving it to you. If you're preoccupied with what you can get, you'll probably end up getting the wrong thing or looking to the wrong people. Plus you'll end up building one of those shallow professional networks that are basically just built around business cards. Those kinds of networks rarely amount to much, because they aren't based upon a principle of generosity. They don't cultivate harmony, so they don't offer people much in the way of real support."

Carlos, Cathie, Jim, and Erica have a profound understanding of the importance of webs and the role they can play in today's VUCA environment. They know that by broadening our links with the world, we can create the opportunities we will need when our circumstances undergo a sudden change or reversal. They also know that building links and creating a sus-

taining web can be highly rewarding in itself. Today's economy does not reward those who insist upon standing alone. The
broader and stronger our webs, the more opportunities we will
create—for ourselves, but also for others.

7

Strategy Five:
Build a Clear Brand

Jim Rosenberg (Mr. Monologue) stresses the importance of creating a strong identity—of *occupying your space*—in order to thrive in the new world of work. But having a strong identity is a twofold proposition. In Chapter 3, we explored strategies for gaining a deeper understanding of your bedrock values. And we looked at how your core influences the choices that you make.

That's the internal part of the process: coming to know yourself. How you *manifest* that sense of yourself in the external world is the second part of the equation. It is not enough merely to know yourself, although it is essential. You also need to be able to project your identity, your self-definition, your personal essence in the public realm. And you need to do so in a way that is powerful, distinctive, authentic, and advantageous.

The manifestation of individual authenticity has been called *personal branding.* Tom Peters pioneered the phrase in his groundbreaking *Fast Company* article "Brand You." In that piece, he urged individuals to start thinking of themselves as if they were brands competing for positions in the marketplace. He noted that in an environment dominated by rapid career shifts and constant instability, each of one of us must define, identify, and represent our own brand, which is ultimately of more consequence than the brand of whatever organization for which we might presently be working. For it is our own individual brand that we carry with us throughout the course of our lives, our own individual brand that evolves and (we hope) grows stronger as we gain more experience and make broader connections.

It was an arresting idea, and it elicited a lot of comment in the form of letters, editorials, and website hits. Some readers thought it was a great approach—useful, timely, clear, and sharp. Others derided the notion of "Brand You" for treating individuals as if they were mere commodities to be bought and traded, and personal identity as something to be manipulated for marketplace gain. Those who felt this way tended to dismiss personal branding as an ultimately soulless and reductive approach to life, one that undervalues the richness and variety of human experience. As one dissenter wrote, "I am not a tube of toothpaste, and refuse to treat myself as if I am!"

However, if we think of personal branding simply as *the means we use to publicly express our core values,* this potential for soullessness and overcommercialization is diffused. If we start from our authentic core, if we think through who we are and what exactly it is that we want to be known for, our capacity to establish a strong and original brand will not be compromised by gimmicks. It will instead become a tool for demonstrating what is most true about ourselves, so we can attract those who want to participate in our life's mission.

This kind of branding is not a reflection of cynicism. It is a reflection of integrity. It's a way of making our work a meaningful expression of ourselves and a way of finding meaning in our work.

This kind of branding is established through our actions and our conversation. Our actions reveal themselves in our daily practice, how we do the things we do. Our conversations link us to others and manifest our identity in words. As Alan Webber, the founder of *Fast Company,* has observed, "The most important work in the new economy is *creating conversations.* Good conversations are about *identity.* They reveal who you are to others. And for that reason, they depend on bedrock human qualities: authenticity, character, integrity. In the end, conversation comes down to trust."

A powerful instance of personal branding through practice was described to me by Marshall Goldsmith, founder of The Learning Network. While working with a Japanese client, Marshall spent time in Kyoto. The hotel where he was staying assigned a guide to show him around. Marshall says, "This guy went out of his way on everything. He extended himself for me at every turn. It was all way beyond the call of duty. At the end of my stay, I told him what a great job he had done. And you know what he said? He said, 'It's not my job. It's my *honor.*'"

Honor gets to the crux of it: honor and passion and ethics and behavior. This is why powerful branding must always reflect an inner commitment. Symbols and design can help you to project who you would *like* to be, but in the end they will fool no one if what you present has nothing to do with your real essence or is contradicted by your actions and your conversation.

Branding manifests itself in four ways:

- ❖ Branding is in your practice
- ❖ Branding is in your materials
- ❖ Branding is in your design
- ❖ Branding is in your symbols

Branding is in your practice

Barbara Roberts, the CEO of Acoustiguide, believes that the strongest way to establish a coherent personal brand is to set rules for *how* you practice your work and then to stick with them over time. "You can't just come up with some slogan about yourself and imagine it means you've got a brand," she says. "You've got to know what you stand for, and then make that clear in all your actions. *That's* what your brand is, how you do even little things, the actions that you take. What you stand for, what you defend, what you're willing to let go of. If you look at it that way, your brand is basically about making clear what your ethics and interests are. *That's* what you bring with you from one job to another."

Barbara notes that consistency is essential for establishing a brand based on practice. "For example, through my whole history, I've always been very strong on women's issues—it's part of what I'm known for, part of how I've established my reputation. This interest started very early, probably when I led a strike of the girls in my second-grade class because we weren't allowed to carry the flag!"

Barbara points out that when she first went to Wall Street,

she established *from day one* that she was there in part because she wanted to make things better for women. She recalls, "I was a child of the sixties. I wasn't all that interested in business; I went to Wall Street to please my father. So that's how I dealt with it: by taking on this mission, by becoming an activist on the job. I was very outspoken about it, and that didn't help me at all in the beginning. It wasn't a popular approach in the early seventies, when there were very few women in the investment banking world, and those that were tended to be silent and put up with whatever came their way. Like having to use the *back staircase,* which is what happened to me."

Barbara's commitment to women's issues made her highly visible. She joined a professional network, Financial Women of New York, and became an activist within it. She was elected president of the group and pushed it to establish links with other women's organizations that had political and social agendas. "I was very flamboyant and outspoken, but always with a purpose. To be truthful, I think part of my insistence and flamboyance came because I wanted to get attention—for myself and for other women—and part of it came because I enjoyed giving people trouble about it! I like stirring things up, it's part of who I am. I'm a provocateur who gets things *done.* It works for me because it's authentic, it is something I care about. My concern and my methods are reflections of my passion."

Barbara notes that while her passion has remained constant, a continually evolving aspect of her brand, she has found new ways to put that energy into practice as time has passed and her position in the world has changed. Upon leaving Wall Street, she undertook an extensive job search. Her goal was to

find a CEO position at a small company that she could grow
and that would give her scope to extend her commitments and
her ideas. The connections she had forged through the years—
on nonprofit boards, with arts groups, dealing with women's issues—had given her prominence, connections, and a strong
brand.

When she was recruited to head FPG, a stock photo
agency, she says, "I *really* got a chance to put my ideas into
practice. That's because as CEO, you set the tone. When I took
over, the company had very few women, no blacks, everybody
looked the same. I made a big push that we were going to have
a highly diverse staff *and* a highly diverse product. We were
going to create an inventory of very diverse images. In every
talk I gave, I stressed that this was our strength, that our diversity enabled us to serve a lot of markets that had been under-
served. The emphasis on diversity of all kinds is an extension
of my commitment to women. It's who I am, but it's also what
I am known for."

Ideas and commitments are part of your practice, but the
day-to-day details of how you operate are probably the most
significant aspect of branding. Erica Gruen, the former Food
Network CEO, is explicit about this. She says, "I very definitely think of myself as the Erica Gruen brand. But I believe
my branding is most apparent in how I *do* things, in the common threads that bind my actions together."

Like Barbara, Erica believes that being consistent is the
most crucial aspect of establishing your brand in practice. "I

don't think you so much *create* a brand as you *establish* one over time. That is, you become a brand because your actions, your behavior, and the way you speak form a consistent pattern. People recognize this, but it takes time before that happens. You can't build a brand overnight."

Erica has built her brand based on a constellation of qualities that define how she does things. "I'm very conscious about the rules of my brand," she says. She describes these as follows:

"I am open to people. I will give you a hearing. I will return your phone call or your e-mail promptly. And yes, I will have lunch with you, at least once. And I will help you if I can, or try to pass you along to someone else."

"I connect people, help them find partners for their ideas. I share the people in my network. And I don't charge for this or take a commission if two people I put together start a business. It's part of who I am, part of how I extend my web."

"I am a spokesperson. I look for opportunities to put myself forward, to speak at events, to be on panels, to talk to the media. I take this seriously and prepare in advance. If you ask me to speak, I will do a good job. I use language, and my voice, in a thoughtful way."

"I have an innate interest in other people's ideas, thoughts, and stories. I do a lot of listening. I want to know what drives people. I'm interested in the inner dynamics, what makes people who they are. That's why I originally became a psychologist. And that's what makes me a good marketer."

Erica adds, "I really think that branding—personal branding anyway—is ultimately about ethics. Ethics is how you *behave*. It's not so much what you believe, but how you act upon

it. People can always tell a personal brand that's authentic, because it matches the person's actions. And they can tell if it's
dishonest because it isn't consistent with how the person really acts."

Branding is in your materials

Branding is implicit in what Bill Taylor, publisher of *Fast
Company* magazine, says when he talks about how people define loyalty today (see Chapter 4). He explains that "people today are loyal to their purpose, loyal to whatever it is that they
are trying to design, loyal to the individuals they work with,
loyal to a certain *way* of working, loyal to a *process*." We explored in Chapter 4 how this loyalty to design and process is
similar to the approach that artists use in their work. And we
saw how artists usually find their individual style *at the same
time* that they find "their" materials.

For visual artists, materials can be paints, scraps of cloth or
wood, sheets of steel, aerosol cans filled with acrylic, pieces of
pipe. The materials artists choose to use, and the particular way
in which they use them, constitutes the brand.

For writers, the prime material is language—the content, or
what they write about, and the particular words that they select.
If their words have a recognizable rhythm, an individual style,
and if they have made certain subjects "theirs," they have a
brand.

For musicians, the prime materials are the instrument they
play and the music that they choose. If they have a distinct
physical relationship with their instrument, and play it in a rec-

ognizable way, and if the kind of music they choose is consistent, they have a brand.

The role of materials in creating a brand has long been recognized in the creative arts. But in the knowledge economy, we can all benefit from approaching our work in a similar way.

If you are a webmaster, your material is the site you create: how it works, how it looks, how it feels to the people who use it. For your brand to be effective, the sites you design should have a consistent look and feel.

If you are the editor of a Latin American business newsletter, your material is your knowledge and understanding of the region, the contacts you have there, your relationships with the writers and designers whose work you present. For your brand to be effective, the way you orchestrate this material should be consistent and identifiable.

If you are the director of training for a financial services company, your material is the programs you devise and the people and technologies you use to deliver them. For your brand to be effective, your programs must have a particular point of view, a distinctive rhythm, a conceptual framework that reveals them as your own.

If you are a caterer, your material is the food you make and serve. For your brand to be effective, the look and taste of what you deliver should reflect your devotion to specific techniques and ingredients.

If you are the manager of a sales team, your material is your relationships with team members and the style of all your communications with them. For your brand to be effective, your voice to the team must have a strong identity.

If you are a high-school teacher, your material is your understanding of your subject, your beliefs about it, and your rapport with your students. For your brand to be effective, you must create a class environment in which your passion for your subject becomes contagious.

Branding requires thought and strategy, a deliberate approach to your materials. So you need to ask yourself some questions:

- What materials do you use in your work?
- How do you use them?
- Why have you chosen these materials?
- To what extent have you made them yours?

Pamela Auchincloss is an independent curator who creates traveling art exhibits for regional and university museums. It's a distinctive niche she created for herself after the Soho gallery she founded closed in the mid-1990s, when the market for contemporary art went into collapse. Pamela's gallery had been known for having a clearly identifiable point of view, representing her distinctive taste in painting. As she herself says, "It was a relatively small gallery, but its presence was great and it had a strong reputation." As befits a woman who pays a lot of attention to the importance of presence and reputation, Pamela has a thoughtful grasp of how materials can be used to build a strong brand.

Pamela opened her first gallery in Santa Barbara, California, when she was twenty-three. She remembers, "I didn't have a real strong feeling about what I was doing, and I didn't have a clear idea of what I liked. My main impetus was wanting to have my own business. I had always been around art, so that seemed like the right place to start. Then I met an older artist, and he educated me about how to look at abstract painting, and I responded to it in a very strong way." Pamela had studied ceramics in Japan, and had been influenced by the Japanese aesthetic, which is highly abstract and focused on materials. "Japan had shaped my sensibilities, helped me to see in abstract terms, so I was basically prepared. I became passionate about abstract painting."

And so she became a woman with a mission: to represent and promote abstract painting. She took that desire with her when she moved to New York. At that time, in the mid-1980s, there wasn't much interest in that kind of work, but Pamela figured that her devotion to it would enable her to create a niche. "The other galleries were showing a little of this, a little of that, whatever everyone else was showing. I was different, I didn't move with the market. The work in my gallery had a strong style, a clear identity. This gave me an advantage in terms of establishing a *presence*. People who liked a certain thing knew they could find it in my gallery." The stable of painters Pamela chose to represent manifested that style.

Pamela did not restrict her efforts to artists who were part of her stable. "Part of my reputation was that I would champion an artist just because I believed in his or her work, because it was consistent with what I liked and wanted to show. So I would make connections for people I didn't represent and help to promote their work. I was approachable—unusual in the New York art world! But I grew up in Oklahoma and Colorado, and people felt they could talk to me. I made studio visits, I offered highly personal service. That's something that I learned in Japan, too, where service is considered part of your brand." Pamela believes that her reputation for having consistent tastes (as well as consistent business practices) gave her a strong advantage in setting up her current business. "I differentiate myself as an exhibition manager *with a point of view.*"

Pamela Auchincloss's materials were her own eye, the physical space her gallery occupied, and her stable of painters. Now that she no longer has a gallery, her materials are more diffuse: the spaces offered by the regional and university museums that are her clients, the shows she custom-builds for them, the context of those shows, the monographs she has published for them. But her distinctive, recognizable taste and eye, along with her reputation and her business practices, are also her materials. Together, they constitute her very recognizable brand.

Branding is in your design

A strong visual design is of course one of the most powerful elements in building a brand. The shape of a Coke bottle, the pure white rectangle of Ivory soap, the bright primary colors and weighty enamel of the KitchenAid standing mixer, the dense line drawings in the old *Children's Illustrated Classics:* All are well-known examples of consistent and strong brand design. Of course, as individuals, we don't have the kind of design resources to build our brands that the great consumer products companies have always had. But we can adapt some of the same principles, using physical design as another means of telling our story.

Once again, the key is authenticity. The physical designs we use will be powerful, not necessarily because they in themselves are great but because they reflect our own sensibility while echoing and supporting what we as individuals stand for. Using design to establish a coherent personal brand is not a matter of inventing a visual slogan but rather encapsulating who we are in a vital and visually accessible way.

Cathie Walker, the founder of amused.com, is very deliberate about using design elements to build her personal brand. She says, "I've always done needlework and sewing projects, and that experience has turned out to be incredibly valuable in helping me to design my website and my business. I believe that how you design your website—how you use design to establish yourself—should always be a clear reflection of *you*."

Cathie points out that her website looks like her house. "It's all primary and pastel colors, very soft and cheerful and inviting. These are also the colors that I wear, the colors that I like, the colors that I feel represent me. The content I use on the site *sounds* like me—very fast and full of ideas, kind of all over the place, but also very creative. When I post new content, I always use my first draft instead of working it over, so that it will sound the way I talk, as if it's all just bursting out of me—which it is! And when someone comes onto my site, I always give them something to do—fill out a questionnaire, join a game, enter a contest. Again, that's what I do when someone comes over to my house. I hand visitors a pack of cards or give them a new toy someone has sent me. I don't just plunk them down in front of the TV!"

Cathie believes that individuals can make powerful use of graphic design even if they don't have the resources to commission custom work. The key, again, is knowing clearly who you are and finding work that projects your essence, that represents you in visual terms.

She says, "I originally purchased the graphic design for my site from Adobe. It was clip art, off the rack—I couldn't afford anything else—but I loved the work. It seemed to be just what I would do if I could draw, so in that way it reflected and represented *me*. Well, I wanted to meet the artist and work more closely with him, so I tracked him down on the Internet. It took a while, but I finally found his e-mail address. So I just sent a note telling him I loved what he did and inviting him to come hang out with me here in Victoria. The idea was just come, let's get to know each other and see if we can do some work together."

Cathie used her strategy of the gift, which we explored in Chapter 6, to cement her relationship with the artist. "I promoted his work to a lot of other websites, and I plugged him into my network. All that brought him a lot of work. Now he's designing everything from my mascot to my kitchen tiles. He even made the wallpaper border for my office, because I like my work space to look like my website and my website to look like my work space." In the same way that Barbara Roberts insists that your practice must be consistent if you are to build a personal brand, so Cathie Walker maintains that your design must be consistent as well.

Cathie is often asked to help with website design. She remarks, "It's amazing how many people don't view the Internet as an opportunity to represent who they actually *are*, to establish a presence in a strong and authentic way. Instead, they want to use the technology to try to reinvent themselves as something they are *not*. And so they either assume a fake identity, or they try to imitate someone else with a successful site. In either case, it's not going to work." Cathie views inauthentic or imitative websites as a lost opportunity to clarify one's personal brand in the marketplace—and as an indication of a kind of fatal fakery. "I mean, you wouldn't answer your own front door in a fright wig, wearing a mask and using a fake name, would you? So why would you try to be someone else on the Internet?"

Jean Bellas, a designer based in Oakland, California, who specializes in creating imaginative work spaces, echoes what Cathie Walker has to say. Jean believes that the Internet provides an unprecedented opportunity for individuals to establish their own brand, using websites and creating their own patterns of hyperlinks. But she also emphasizes that *process* is the most powerful element in the design of a personal brand.

If you want to stand out in a crowded marketplace, says Jean, you must design a distinctive *way* of working that captures attention and clarifies what you have to offer, while also creating identifiable value for your team or company. And that process must be reflected in how you design your work.

Jean's observations about branding by means of a distinctive *process* connect with Barbara Roberts's understanding of branding as the result of *practice,* as well as Cathie Walker's emphasis on visual design. Indeed, Jean views practice as an essential aspect of design. "The more conscious your practice is, the more designed it will be," she says. "And the more designed it is, the more it will distinguish you in the marketplace. Your process is what makes what you do *you.*"

Jean believes that your individual design process derives from four things:

- How you interact with the community of which you are a part—your organization, your colleagues, but most especially your immediate team
- How you use technology to your advantage
- How you foster and develop your own capacity for innovation—how you do R&D
- How you organize your time and your physical space

Clearly, Cathie Walker has given careful attention to the role that her process plays in shaping her design. I was also reminded of Dorothy Brunson, the Baltimore radio station owner I profiled in *The Female Advantage* (mentioned in Chapter 5) who had two glass-walled offices side-by-side. Dorothy's way of working emphasized her transparency, her accessibility, her humor, and the fact that she saw her jobs as owner and operator as different approaches and different skills. This perception of difference determined how she organized her time. It all added up to a highly distinctive and well-designed approach.

Branding is in your symbols

Cathie Walker stuck a Mr. Potato Head on her website when she built it, to establish the "essential silliness" of her enterprise.

Marshall Goldsmith uses his personal slogan, "Life is good," at the end of every phone call and every e-mail. It has proven infectious, and now members of The Learning Network use it among themselves. Marshall's signature phrase has become part of the network's culture.

Julie Anixter showed her enthusiasm for the ASK System

by loading it on to her computer and carrying it wherever she went. When she spoke at a conference or professional gathering, she would switch on the program and demonstrate it. In this way, she expressed her excitement and identified herself with a technology she saw as cutting edge.

Erin Thomas adapted Joan of Arc's white flag as a personal amulet when she decided to switch from marketing to studying for the ministry, and had a pin designed with the image. It symbolizes the surrender of her former self, as well as the high purpose she has found in her new life.

Jim Rosenberg's "handle" of Mr. Monologue not only defines what he does but has become his personal signature, as well as an affectionate way of describing his family.

Images, amulets, personal sign-offs, logos, mantras: all of these are symbols. They can be a powerful, nonverbal means for communicating what you are about. They can be distinctive, or they can be typical, a shorthand way of conjuring up an image, a way of describing who in the world you are.

A huge website for job-hunters recently posted a listing from a young woman looking for interesting work. She wrote, "If you see someone dashing around with a coffee cup in one hand and a phone in the other, you'll know it's me. I simply *must* always be doing three things at once, and I never sit still." The image described her in vivid, though not particularly unique, terms. She received a lot of inquiries.

Throughout this book, we have examined the extent to which the working habits and techniques traditionally used by

artists, musicians, and writers have become useful for all of us
in a knowledge economy. This is because a knowledge economy puts a premium on creativity and emphasizes the contribution and uniqueness of the individual. Artists, musicians, and
writers have throughout history been known by their processes,
their use of materials, and their approach to design. *How they
use these has defined their uniqueness.* But the most popular
and successful creative people have always also had a signature, a symbolic shorthand that enabled them to lodge their image in the public's consciousness—a way of saying in five
seconds *This is who I am.*

Louis Armstrong's signature was closing his sets with the
simple and elegiac song "It's a Wonderful World." It made
clear in five seconds that he was an optimist, a man who loved
life against the odds, and that jazz, of which he was the ambas-
sador, was a music of buoyancy and hope.

Jackson Pollock's signature was the canvas looped with
paint drips. It made clear in five seconds that his work resulted
from a series of improvised physical acts rather than a plan
drawn up in advance, and that "action art" was a manifestation
of personal boldness, a high-wire act.

Ernest Hemingway's signature was the brief declarative
sentence, stripped bare of adjectives and ornament. It made
clear in five seconds that he was in rebellion against all that
was ornate, convoluted, and insincere, and that he represented
a more direct and modern aesthetic.

These artistic giants had signatures that enabled their listeners, viewers, and readers to instantly identify the sensibility that
lay behind a work. Because of their signatures, these artists

were able to establish their personal brands in the most power-ful, and easily identifiable, possible way.

In a crowded marketplace, your personal signature is a manifestation of your brand. Your brand is established by your practice, your materials, the elements of design you use, and the symbols that you choose to represent yourself. When you are creating a personal brand, all of your actions and all of your words *count*. Being careless about them dilutes your presenta-tion. If it is to be powerful, personal branding must outwardly manifest what lies at your inner core. If your brand fails to re-flect your essence, you might as well answer the door in a fright wig, as Cathie Walker reminds us.

Our conversation is the link between our brand and our au-thenticity. As Alan Webber pointed out earlier in this chapter, good conversations are about identity, about revealing who you are to others. Speaking authentically and with integrity inspires trust.

And the true value of great brands is that people trust them.

8
Strategy Six:
Practice the Rhythm
of Renewal

We all know the reasons that life in 24/7 can be tough, despite the opportunities it presents.

It's tough because of the multiplicity of choices we all face.

It's tough because we must continually reinvent our lives as our organizations and our opportunities evolve.

It's tough because technologies that operate at a speed beyond human consciousness are reshaping how we do our work.

It's tough because these same technologies are everywhere, which means we are subject to constant interruptions.

It's tough because the old division of labor between the sexes is breaking down, which means that most of us must manage both workplace and domestic concerns.

Many of us have tried to cope with the pace and keep the inherent stresses at bay by working harder or faster, or by multitasking. But we generally find that these efforts are self-defeating if we resort to them on any consistent basis.

Working harder saps our energies if we do it for more than brief spurts of time. And the intensity it requires of us makes us less creative, less able to innovate. As the late Supreme Court

Justice Louis Brandeis once said, he could get more work done in eleven months than in twelve. We all know that if we're stuck trying to remember the title of a song or the name of an actor, the only remedy is to *stop thinking about it* and wait for the elusive phrase to pop into our mind. Creative thought is like that. It occurs when we are most relaxed, when we are in the frame of mind that psychologists call "flow," deeply absorbed in the task at hand. Thus, working harder month after month in the end has the effect of sabotaging our efforts, since creativity and innovation are what today's economy ultimately rewards.

Working faster leads to sloppy work. It also deprives us of joy in life, for to work at top speed, we have to block out sensory input and concentrate solely upon the task at hand. Again, it is possible to do this in short bursts, but doing it consistently over time costs us, leaving us feeling empty and unsure about the purpose of our lives.

Multitasking is probably the 24/7 strategy that has gained the most attention over the last few years. More and more of us are attempting to compress our work by doing several things at once. Of course, the technology that we use, being cheap, lightweight, and portable, makes accomplishing several things at once easier than in the past. Indeed, *to multitask has become a constant temptation.*

But multitasking *combines* the drawbacks of working harder and working faster. It inhibits creativity, since it is impossible for an extraordinary new idea to pop into a distracted and divided mind. Most of us can all trace some of our best ideas to inspired moments in the bathtub or on a long aimless bike ride, for the brain seems to make its best connections when it's not paying full attention. Multitasking also leads us to sloppy mistakes. We delete a whole speech we were writing because we were also talking on the phone, we burn a piecrust because we were trying to do our e-mail at the same time. And multitasking can quickly make us feel as if we're on a treadmill, functioning merely as instruments for getting through our work. This is because doing work we are not fully *engaged* by is ultimately unsatisfying. And we can't be engaged when we are also doing something else.

Our difficulty coping with the pace of life is exacerbated by the increasing integration of public and private. Though the workplace in the past could often be intense, people were nevertheless usually able to count on being able to relax at home, for their domestic lives (unless some tragedy intervened) were usually fairly free of stress and required relatively few decisions. Today, however, our private lives often feel like highwire acts, for all the reasons we examined in Chapter 2.

As a result, more and more of us are tempted to try to work harder, work faster, and multitask *at home as well as at work.* In doing so, we use professional survival skills to try to bring order and efficiency to our private lives. This, more than anything, is what makes the traditional approach of keeping our noses to the grindstone self-defeating in today's VUCA environment, for buckling down and trying harder at home *and* at work is a recipe for misery and exhaustion.

If the dominant methods for coping with the pace of life are either doomed to failure or take too great a toll on the quality of our lives, how do we manage a rhythm of life that threatens to overwhelm us? How do we keep a grip on what makes us human while asserting our value in the marketplace? How do we retain our sanity and our serenity in a world that sometimes seems designed to undermine us?

First, we need to get real about what's possible.

All too often, we burden ourselves with unrealistic pictures of what life is like for others, and then feel like failures when we don't live up to the standard we think they set. We read stories of executives who manage to raise four children as if they were rolling out of bed, and maintain Martha Stewart homes in the process. We rarely look at the psychological toll this takes, or the toll on relationships. Nor do we consider that the executive probably has a personal assistant as well as a nanny. Instead, we get taken in by the image and wonder where *we* have gone wrong and why *we* can't seem to measure up.

One consequence of having more diverse lives these days is that it has become more difficult to envision exactly what other people's lives are *like*. This leaves us free to project our own imaginings upon them. We need to focus on what *we* want and what *we* can reasonably achieve in the course of a day, and forget what it *seems* like other people are doing. Nor should we be dazzled by the glowing lists of family achievements routinely sent out with holiday greetings, which can lead us to orgies of remorseful comparison. *They* are not *us,* nor are they telling their whole story.

Second, we need to control our lives at work as much as possible.

We must push hard against bosses who require an inhuman pace or set standards that make a mockery of our human need for balance. We need to articulate what we *could* be contributing to our organization if we felt vigorous and refreshed, and we need to demonstrate those potential contributions. We need to stop trying to prove our loyalty and instead concentrate on proving our value.

We also need to understand that our own success at work will largely depend upon our ability to help our boss and our organization recognize what we could ultimately be and do, and to educate them about the best way to enable us to achieve it. If we permit anyone in a temporary position of authority to turn us into a grind, we will not only deprive them of our real value, we will diminish our own value in the broader marketplace. For allowing our individual value to diminish is dangerous in a world in which few organizations are reliably stable over time and none can offer guaranteed employment. And so if we find ourselves in a situation where our organization gives us no room to negotiate a way of working that satisfies us and helps us to reach our potential, we need to think about ways to reinvent the nature of our work (see Chapter 5). Or we need to find another job.

Third, we need to avoid assuming unnecessary burdens.

Dr. Linda Clever, an internist and occupational therapist, tells a story about a physician at Dartmouth College who teaches an ethics class for medical students. One day, the class was discussing the role of stress in causing doctors to make unethical decisions or to engage in compromises that betray their own deep-rooted values. A student remarked, "It seems like you're saying that stress leads to bad decisions. In that case, what's the most important thing I can do to minimize stress in my medical career?" The class listened expectantly for the professor to offer a broad or highly theoretical insight. Instead, he responded simply, "Don't buy a big house!"

"What he was telling them," says Dr. Clever, "was to avoid trapping themselves with heavy financial obligations. That's the number-one reason people compromise their values, the number-one reason people stay in jobs they don't like, the number-one reason people lose touch with what they really want to be doing. I see it too. People burden themselves by assuming financial obligations that then rule the choices that they make. They feel they have to maintain a certain level of spending, and *increase* it as the years go by. They don't really question why they are doing any of this. They tell themselves they've got a good job, they should be able to afford a great house. But what if the nature of their job changes, or the demands become too great, or they decide they don't like what they're doing? If you put yourself in a position where you feel you have to maintain a certain income, you often end up compromising yourself."

Erica Gruen, the Internet consultant, remarked upon the importance of keeping spending down in Chapter 6. She expands upon that by adding, "One thing I've learned through my years of working: frugality is how you buy your freedom! In order to really operate in the new economy, in order to be able to take advantage of opportunities and walk away from a job when it's no longer worth it, you need to have a sense of security. That means living below your income and saving everything you can. It means not caring so much about *things* that you sacrifice your freedom. That's how I've always thought about it. What's more important, a new car or my freedom? And freedom is having some money in the bank. Being flexible is the most important gift you can give yourself today. But you can't be flexible if you're carrying debt or living beyond your means."

Finally, we need to incorporate acts of renewal into our daily lives.

Our days, crammed with a multitude of responsibilities, sometimes seem programmed to exhaust us. As a result, we become focused on simply getting through the day. But, as Linda Clever also observes, "The skills that get us through the day in this environment are not necessarily the same skills that get us through our *lives.* The daily skills are about efficiency and coping, but the lifetime skills are about sustaining ourselves. Now, I'm all in favor of getting through the day! But if we also want to sustain ourselves, we need to take a longer view. We need to think consciously about how we are going to renew ourselves. This means we have to break with our habit of just doing whatever gets us through the day."

Self-renewal, according to Dr. Clever, requires that we disrupt our everyday rhythm. In this way, self-renewal is similar to what takes place in the neutral zone.

Bill Bridges, the psychologist and consultant we met in Chapter 3, describes the neutral zone as "a place where we cease to function in our accustomed way." Because our usual pattern has been disrupted, we perceive entering the neutral zone as being in limbo. Being in limbo is unpleasant but, as Bill points out, spending time in the neutral zone is a way of fostering personal renewal. Bill also notes that entry into the neutral zone is usually initiated by a crisis that forces us to recognize that our usual solutions are no longer working. This recognition leads to a break in our routine, a disruption of our daily habits, a wrench thrown into our tightly drawn schedule. By stepping back from normal life, we have the opportunity to look with fresh eyes at what we are doing and who we are in the world.

Spending time in the neutral zone can be enormously useful when we are wrestling with the core issues of our identity. But it is by nature a special event, an extreme solution. When our concern is *daily* self-renewal, we need less drastic measures. Nevertheless, the fundamental idea is similar. Refreshment of spirit is brought about by disruption, by taking a break from our usual routine. The key is to *find ways to incorporate small breaks or disruptions into our everyday efficient schedule,* so that we can refresh ourselves each day, each week, each month.

How do you practice this kind of fruitful disruption? How can you bring breathing space into your crowded days? How do you fight a world in which everything seems geared to speed and efficiency? There are many many techniques. They include:

❖ Connecting with timeless rhythms
❖ Identifying your sources of joy
❖ Cultivating mindfulness
❖ Incorporating the elements of Slow

Connecting with timeless rhythms

Our primary purpose in working harder, working faster, and multitasking is essentially to beat the clock, for life in VUCA often seems to put us in competition with time itself. To some degree, we perceive time as our enemy. It's the blind force, the great inevitable, against which we wage a daily struggle.

And indeed, it is at least partly true that time (as we typically perceive it) *has* become our enemy, something alien to ourselves. As we saw in Chapter 1, we experience time in two entirely different ways: as the cyclical rhythms of nature, governed by the recurrent seasons; and as the repetitive rhythms of the machine, regulated by schedules, calendars, and the clock. Now that home is no longer a sanctuary, an inviolate retreat from the mechanical measures of work—*and* now that time itself has been speeded up by being broken up into digital units—all of us are governed by mechanical time to a greater extent than at any period in history.

This is the true reason that so many of us feel "out of balance." We in fact *are* unbalanced, since a major aspect of our human nature is being stifled and denied by our attempts to adapt to the unnatural and repetitive rhythms of the machine. Our efforts to adapt to our circumstances undermine our basic human equilibrium. And what is equilibrium if not a sense of balance? The stress we are experiencing is thus more than simply a question of being busy. It is the result of our failing to honor an important aspect of what makes us human—our connection to the natural world. The stress we feel is also a signal that we need to reconnect with the recurrent rhythms of nature. There are two powerful ways to do so, and in the process to disrupt the dominant role the clock plays in our lives.

The first is simply to spend more time in nature, where the timeless rhythms that are the deepest part of our human heritage are alive and manifest at every moment. This means we need to get outdoors whenever we can, eat lunch in the park rather than the cafeteria, take a bike ride after work instead of visiting the health club, hike with our families on weekends instead of going to movies, walk in the mornings as the sun is coming up. It means that we need to lobby our organizations to build roof gardens or outdoor cafés as part of our physical environment and press the professional groups to which we belong to hold at least some part of their seminars and conferences in the out-of-doors, rather than requiring us to travel to magnificent settings so that we can hole up in windowless conference rooms.

As a corollary to these efforts, we must refuse to spend great amounts of our leisure in activities that are governed by the clock—activities in which we need to time ourselves, or that require us to stick to a schedule. We should also get as much sunlight as we can. Dr. Christiane Northrup, the wellness guru, notes that the most powerful antistress hormones are secreted by our pituitary gland, and that this gland is activated *solely* by natural sunlight. She says that the most effective antidote to stress is spending one half hour in natural light (without glasses or sunglasses) every single day. This is yet another reason that we need to get outdoors.

Simply *being* in the natural world disrupts our mechanical relationship with time. But observing nature, or working with it, brings about a far more powerful disruption. Closely watching the birds or the stars or the changing vegetation puts us in sync with natural rhythms, which unfold recurrently and slowly, for these activities demand patience as well as our full attention. Tending plants, flowers, and vegetables—even just puttering in the garden or growing herbs on a windowsill—returns us to our ancient human relationship with time, which follows seasonal and recurrent patterns. And so making more

space for the natural world in our everyday lives is perhaps the
most important way to renew and refresh our clock-battered
spirits.

Participating in traditional rituals is the other great means
of reconnecting with seasonal and recurrent time, for rituals
have their roots in the ancient celebration of the seasons. Our
major holidays, of course, originally derived from these rituals,
but the ways in which we celebrate them have more and more
come to reflect our mechanical approach to time. And so we
rush around making elaborate preparations, drive all over town
to buy people presents, undertake orgies of cooking, or exhaust
selves in airports by choosing to travel at these most hectic
imes. Although our determination to really "do up" the hol-
ys reveals our inner longing to connect with a more cyclical
oroach to time, the *ways* in which we do so often leave us
ling more frazzled, more driven by the clock, less satisfied
d spiritually replenished.

For our holidays to assume their intended role, our celebra-
ons *must disrupt our day-to-day and clock-bound way of being in the world.* They must put us in touch with what is eternal
in our own tradition. And they must become a means of connecting us with what is timeless in the world.

A number of people I interviewed for this book spoke of
having found a way to make this happen. Erica Gruen was particularly eloquent on the subject. She said, "I have a history of
not being good about building in things that renew me, like taking time off or going to the health club or working out. But that

has changed over the last few years. I've built renewal into my life in an unexpected way by becoming more involved with my religion, which is Judaism. I now have a study partner, and she and I read ancient texts together every week. If we can't get together, we discuss them on the phone. It is so incredibly refreshing to be deeply involved with something *not* connected with my daily life, something that has nothing to do with the challenge of balancing the demands of a family while running a business, something completely at odds with the issues of the new economy. What we are studying is unrelated to *anything* in our lives, but instead focuses on those issues that have preoccupied Jewish minds for millennia."

Erica also notes that her studies connect her to childhood memories in a very profound way, and that this has become increasingly important to her as life speeds up. Inspired by the refreshment she has found, Erica has in the last few years begun celebrating the ancient Friday night ritual of the Sabbath with her husband and daughter. "I've stopped scheduling business on Friday afternoons, and I just spend my time getting ready. This has become the main source of my ability to renew myself. My family is connecting to something that is absolutely timeless. And that puts everything else we do in a new perspective."

What Erica has done is to disrupt the patterns that enable her simply to get through the day and substitute rituals that are focused on getting her through her *life*. There are different ways for all of us to do this. We can find refreshment by returning to the ritualized practices of our own tradition, or by studying and practicing rituals from a tradition different from that in which we grew up but which nevertheless have a particular resonance for us. Stanley Siegel, the therapist who spoke insight-fully about the comfort people have today with the idea of self-invention, notes that the need to connect with timeless rituals in a world of constant change is a major reason that so many Americans and Europeans have begun practicing Buddhism, visiting retreat centers, and incorporating meditation into their daily lives.

Meditation, of course, is essentially a disciplined approach to connecting with the moment, for moving beyond obsessive concerns with the past or the future, so that the mind has room to contemplate, to *be* in the present. This is what being in nature also provides. The great landscape designer Russell Page observed that the true pleasure of gardening was to "break the crazy rhythm, to change and stop the rush of time, thus making the garden a quiet island in which *the moment* has new meaning." What Page describes is precisely what we need in an era when constant duties divide our attention. We must find ways of putting ourselves fully *in the present,* because only the eternal present is truly timeless.

Identifying your sources of joy

Barbara Roberts also has strong feelings about how best to seek refreshment in a demanding and fast-paced environment, although her approach is entirely different from Erica's.

Barbara says, "I think the most effective way to renew yourself is to think back to what gave you real joy when you were a child, and then make an effort to incorporate it into your present life. What activities or places excited you and refreshed you as a child? What places gave you a sense of purpose, a sense of belonging in the world? When you can identify *that,* you have the key to creating your own personal means of renewal. Because what gave you joy as a child relates to who you are at the deepest level, and to what your destiny is in the world."

In thinking back upon her own childhood, Barbara realized that she was always at her happiest whenever her family went to the ocean. "That's what I lived for, that's what made everything worthwhile, that's what cheered me up and gave me a sense of freedom and peace. When I realized that, I began to see that the sea has always been the source of my deepest refreshment, the place where I can get in touch with the ground of my being. And so I plan around that knowledge. I take time to go to the sea every three months. I go there when I'm between jobs, when I need time to think or plan. It is my priority. It's something I know I need. It's something I negotiate for in advance."

Barbara also points out that she uses the time she spends at the sea in a highly conscious way, which adds to its potential for renewal. She says, "When I sit on a beach, I very deliberately take the time to reconnect with my childhood. I remember back, think deeply about what it was like for me being a child, about what feelings and observations formed me." By connecting the time she now spends at the sea with remembrances of how she felt as a child, she finds a level of refreshment that is truly profound.

This conscious approach is key to incorporating the rhythm of renewal into our lives, enabling us to connect with our own most essential being. For it is both the conscious act *and* the

sense of connection to our own past that breaks our habit of focusing on simply *getting through the day* and puts us in touch
with the larger purpose of our life.

If you want to identify the sources of your own joy, you can
start by asking yourself some questions:

- What did you most enjoy doing with your family as a
  child?
- What did you most enjoy doing alone?
- What gave you a sense of freedom and independence?
- What gave you a sense of mastery and power?
- What gave you an appreciation for the mystery and
  beauty of the world?
- What made you feel connected to something larger than
  yourself?

Once you have a clear picture of what engaged your spirit
in childhood, you will have a more powerful understanding of
what might renew you by connecting you to your deepest self.
Perhaps overnight scouting trips inspired you, as they did
Katherine Armstrong's husband. Or maybe, like the art dealer
Pamela Auchincloss, you felt most at peace when riding a
horse. Or maybe the freedom of just jumping on a bike and going for a long ride alone seemed to unlock something in your
spirit. Whatever solaced and excited you when you were young
provides a clue about what you might do now to renew and refresh yourself today.

The idea here is *not* to attempt to recapture the past. As we
have noted, true renewal takes place when one is *fully in the
moment.* The idea is to identify those activities that can return

us to the moments that imprinted us most deeply and joyfully in our early lives—and then to make room for those experiences in our everyday present.

Cultivating mindfulness

Multitasking by definition requires that we *fragment* our attention by focusing on several different things at the same time. Multitasking is thus the ideal means for putting ourselves *out* of sync with the present moment. We have already seen that multitasking often leads to sloppy work, inhibits creativity, and can make us feel as if we are mere instruments whose only purpose in life is to complete our tasks. But in addition to all this, multitasking also undermines the rhythm of renewal.

True renewal requires the *disruption* of our everyday efficient schedule to engage more fully with the present. This enables us to experience our lives instead of just using our energies to make it through the day. Multitasking, by contrast, intensifies our everyday patterns rather than disrupting them. It takes us away from the moment, which we are powerless to experience, since it is impossible for us to be fully present when our minds are in two places at once. The more energy we devote to multitasking, the less ability we will have to refresh ourselves. This is perhaps the most important reason that we should try to avoid it.

People in the Western world have known since the 1979 publication of Dr. Herbert Benson's best-selling *The Relaxation Response* that being fully engaged with the moment is the best way to relieve everyday stress. Thanks in part to Dr.

Benson's influence, millions of people in the last two decades have taken up various kinds of meditation as a way of connecting to the moment. Most of the meditative techniques we use have been adapted from Eastern practice. There is great variety among them, but almost all incorporate exercises that enable us to become more conscious of our breath in order to reconnect to the present moment.

However, there is no way that we can breathe consciously when we are multitasking. There is no way we can talk on the phone while scanning through e-mail and still maintain an awareness of our breath slowly coming in and going out. There is no way we can coordinate our breath with our movements when we are dictating correspondence or watching the television news while on the treadmill. The whole point of breathing exercises is to bring us to awareness. And when we do several things at once, we cannot be fully aware of any one thing. We are by definition, and by choice, scattered.

The rhythm of renewal demands that we cultivate mindfulness—a continual awareness of what we are doing at each moment in time. Eastern meditation experts have many techniques for enabling us to achieve this. For example, Thich Nhat Hanh, a Vietnamese monk, advocates that whenever we hear a telephone ring, we stop whatever we are doing for a few seconds and take one long deep breath. We can *then* go ahead and answer the phone if we wish to do so. The bell acts as a cue, recalling us to ourselves, disrupting the pattern of our everyday unconscious awareness.

Thich Nhat Hanh remarks that using the telephone in this way is similar to how people throughout history have used temple and church bells: as a subtle reminder that draws their awareness to the present moment and turns their thoughts to the larger meaning of their lives. As such, something as mundane and distracting as the phone can become a tool for incorporating small but persistent acts of renewal into our everyday lives.

Of course, we can't remember to take a deep breath when the phone rings if the sound catches us doing three things at once. Avoiding multitasking as much as possible is probably *the* most important thing we can do to foster our own renewal and build a less grinding rhythm into our every day. This is particularly important when we are exercising, for exercising should be a means for refreshing not only our bodies but our minds and our spirits as well.

Incorporating the elements of Slow

The strong, and much publicized, European backlash against genetically engineered food has sparked a continent-wide movement that offers some powerful insights for those of us seeking to connect with the rhythm of renewal. Many Europeans have come to believe that the most effective response to the development of what they call "frankenfood" lies ultimately in the deliberate cultivation of the "philosophy of Slow."

The philosophy of Slow is most clearly manifested in the Slow Food Movement, which is now an international membership organization with a sophisticated website and a quarterly magazine published simultaneously in six languages. The Slow Food Movement takes as its starting point the conviction that, in a technologically advanced world, we can best resist the pressures of globalization and the pace imposed by digital technologies by searching out the "traces of humanity" that exist in traditional approaches to cuisine.

As a result, the Slow Food Movement promotes and exalts foods that take a long time to produce and dishes that take a long time to prepare. It also champions foods that reflect the particular place in which they have been grown and nurtured. The Slow Food Movement thus presents itself as the antithesis of the fast food phenomenon. It is a subtle means of resistance tailored to surviving in a world in which we all feel the pressure to work harder and faster and to multitask.

What does this mean for those of us trying to incorporate acts of renewal into our everyday lives?

Potentially, quite a lot. The philosophy of Slow proposes a counterintuitive approach to the speeded-up demands of life in 24/7. Instead of attempting to meet them by matching the hectic pace they seem to demand, we *slow ourselves down.* Instead of trying to figure out ways to do more things more quickly, we deliberately pursue activities that require us to slacken our pace. If we like cooking, we spend whatever free hours we can manage simmering long-cooking and complexly flavored stews. If we like building cabinets, we learn to use a lathe rather than buzzing the surface of the wood with a power tool. If we like gardening, we plant from seed and summon the patience to watch our plants grow over the course of the season.

Similarly, if we have a child, we needn't feel we must constantly dash from zoo to puppet stand to children's museum on a Saturday to ensure that we are spending quality time with our son or daughter. Instead, we might spend a quiet afternoon with our child baking gingerbread cookies or building a model airplane or planting carrot seeds in a careful row in the backyard. By doing so, we can enjoy immersing ourselves in a complex but relaxing activity with our child, rather than rushing him or her from one activity to the next. And we can teach our child that it is fine to enjoy such pleasures.

Of course, we might argue that we don't have free time to use in *any* fashion, much less squandering precious hours over a complicated stew. But the principles of Slow can also be incorporated into our work as well as into our leisure activities, for at heart the philosophy of Slow is basically about a refusal to hurry. And we *can* refuse to hurry in most situations, except those involving actual life and death. For most of us, hurry has become a habit. At work, it is a way of demonstrating our loyalty rather than proving our value, and as such it can be self-defeating.

Years ago, when I used to be a speechwriter for executives, I quickly developed the ability to recognize the most senior people when they appeared at any event. They did not carry coats, even when it was cold or raining, because they had a driver or assistant to take care of such things. And, most recognizably, *they never hurried.* The people around them hurried as a way of trying to prove their usefulness and their willingness to do the boss's bidding. But the senior executives never so much as quickened their pace. The way they carried themselves reflected their conviction that they had value, their belief that they had absolutely nothing to prove.

Over the last decade, many hierarchies have flattened and more and more of us have proven adept at creating our work, carving out our niches, defining our value. But too many of us have kept the old underlying habit of rushing through our daily paces, as if we had no independence and must constantly prove ourselves. Very often, we imagine that we will be rewarded for behaving in this way, and of course sometimes we are. But by constantly hurrying, we not only poison the quality of our individual lives, we also undermine our own ultimate value by adopting a demeanor that suggests we are at someone else's beck and call, rather than moving through life comfortably, at our own pace, in accord with our own inner rhythm and light.

But how can we overcome our habit of hurrying? Where can we find the confidence to slow down? Two sources of help are easily available.

First, some of the most effective methods for combating the tendency to hurry can be found in the practice and literature of cognitive therapy. This is a branch of psychology that emphasizes the power of the rational mind to determine our behavior. The guiding notion is that our feelings are determined by our thoughts. If we work to change our thoughts, we can also change our feelings. And so we must ask ourselves:

- Why are we hurrying?
- What specific reasons make us believe that doing so is necessary?
- Who are we afraid will be angry or disappointed if we take more time?
- Would he or she really be that upset if we paced ourselves?
- If he or she would be very upset, what would that mean for us?
- What is the worst thing that could happen if we did not hurry?

As we ask these questions, we uncover both conscious and unconscious assumptions that influence how we behave. We might recognize, for example, that the reason we are hurrying is that we think that our boss is about to fire us, and we want to try to prove how necessary we are. If we bring this thought to light, it spurs more questions. *Why* do we believe we are about to be fired? Is the company downsizing our division? If so, will hurrying really prevent our own dismissal? If instead we believe that our boss is just looking for an excuse to move us out of the picture, will hurrying really prevent this from happening? Might there be a more effective way for us to prove our value? Are we trying to cover up for a lack of skills that we are worried will be discovered? If so, how might we upgrade or acquire these skills?

Asking such questions can be a powerful exercise—a means for uncovering what lies at our core, for exposing unexamined fears and hopes we have about our jobs, our relationships, our lives. Of course, we are not talking here about working swiftly to complete a particular project; we are talking about compulsive hurrying, which is a problem for many of us and has become a habit in many workplaces.

A second source of help when we need to slow down is recognizing the limits of our own efforts, for we often hurry because we imagine that doing so will compel an outcome that really lies beyond our control. Chris Cappy, the president of Pilot Consulting who talked about doing a yearly self-audit, says he used to hurry for this reason. But something he learned while studying meditation enabled him to stop.

One day, a guru with whom Chris was working saw how he was struggling with his practice and drew him out about his problems. The guru concluded that Chris was simply trying too hard. He then said something that ultimately changed Chris's approach not only to his meditation but to his work. The guru said, "Every bird flies with two wings. He flies with the wing of self-effort, but also with the wing of grace."

We hurry because we do not believe that we are supported by the wing of grace but must instead rely solely upon our own efforts. We hurry because we do not trust in grace.

When we *stop* hurrying, we acknowledge our own limits. We surrender to the universe. And in doing so, we open ourselves to the rhythm of renewal. And renewal is what we most crave and seek when we have been flying too long on the single wing of self-effort. Restoration and renewal come only when we leave aside the struggle and permit ourselves to rely on the wing of grace.

As Chris Cappy says, "I now keep this constantly in mind. On any given project, there is only so much I can do, only so much responsibility I can assume, only so much of an effort I can make. I am always aware now that a part of me is relying on grace."

Grace, mindfulness, and slowness renew us, whereas effort, distraction, and hurry exhaust us. We must find ways to make room for what renews us in our daily lives. And we must insist on incorporating it into how we do our work.

Conclusion:
The Tao of Now

The conditions of life are more intense in our world today. The conditions of work are more intense as well.

They are not *tougher* than they were in years past. They are not bleaker, certainly not more painful. Nor are they so discouraging. They rarely threaten to trap us on a treadmill of unceasing labor. Nor do they require our mindless obedience, as the conditions of work so often did in the industrial era.

We are less tied to organizations, less dependent upon them than we used to be. Thus, we are more free to make our own choices—choices that reflect our individual wants and requirements.

Perhaps most important, *our talents and ideas are needed as never before.* The economy, and thus the workplace, are being shaped by what we have to offer, by how we respond to the challenges of every day.

And yet, the world that shapes our lives is volatile, uncertain, complex, and ambiguous. It is in consequence profoundly demanding. The range of choices that confronts us can seem overwhelming. The rules by which most of us grew up no longer apply. Long-cherished values struggle to find an honored place. The press of tasks and duties leaves us less time to *think,* unless we commit ourselves to making that a priority. Yet the need to make constant decisions requires us to spend more time in thought.

As circumstances evolve under the influence of forces we can seek to understand but cannot control, we find that we must improvise, making up our lives as we go along. This is not because we have mislaid the script or somehow misunderstood it. It's because there *is* no script. Our personal narrative is whatever we make it, shaped by circumstance, whim, and resolve.

Because both work and life are so demanding, creating ways of working and living that meet our individual needs has become more necessary to our well-being than ever. Work consumes more of our time and more of our attention. As a result, *enjoying* our work has become more critical to our satisfaction than it was for people in years past. It's harder to resign ourselves to doing work that doesn't interest us when we have to harness so much energy and intelligence to do it.

It is not only difficult, it is also self-defeating for us to reconcile ourselves to earning a living by doing that which does not engage us. This is because *it is impossible to be intuitive about that which does not compel our interest.* Nurturing, developing, and honoring our intuition is the key to survival in an era of constant change because intuition enables us to recognize and sense what is coming next. This simple fact *requires* us to search out or create ways of working that reflect our individual interests and give full scope to our talents.

Improvisation and intuition are the most important adaptive skills of the era into which we have been born. Only intuition can enable us to meet an uncertain future. Only by improvising can we make the most of circumstances that are continually in flux.

There has been a lot of talk in the last few years about the role of spirit in the workplace. Many people believe this emphasis is misplaced. They prefer the old model, which held spirit as the proper concern of private life, with economic values and goals governing the domain of work. But the need to be intuitive and to improvise has made this kind of compartmentalization obsolete, bringing the concerns of spirit squarely into the world of work.

Why is this so?

First, because intuition unites what we logically *know* with what our deepest core *senses*. It thus draws upon the realm of spirit, which is what links us to our deepest core.

Second, because improvisation is the means by which we put what we intuit coming next *into action.* To connect with our sense of what is coming next, we must tap the wellspring of spirit.

In jazz, the art form that elevates improvisation to an aesthetic principle, the skilled improviser is one who is able to connect his or her individual intuition of how a given sequence of notes should unfold with the intuition of the larger group, creating a sense of communion. Intuition and improvisation thus reveal themselves in jazz as two aspects of the same impulse.

So it is in our lives. So should it be in our work.

In an environment that changes all the time and is too rich with choice, each one of us is thrown back upon our inmost resources. We must wrestle with the challenge of composing a life that suits our specific and individual requirements, rather than becoming distracted by the wealth of options that is available to us. The very multiplicity of options forces us to choose.

Our intuition is our surest guide to identifying our requirements and to making wise choices.

These choices then manifest themselves in our daily improvisations.

This is why the realm of the spirit can no longer be kept distinct from our lives at work. We need a kind of guidance that exists beyond the realm of pure logic to forge and create our individual way, our personal path.

The notion of way or path is expressed in Chinese culture by the great, ancient concept of the *Tao*. The Tao of Now—the *way* of our era—is the *path* of change. Those among us who recognize this and understand its implications will be best positioned to exercise influence upon our surroundings and so shape our lives in ways that are meaningful and appropriate. In determining how to do this, traditional Chinese wisdom has much to teach us.

In his translation of the classic *Tao Te Ching,* R. W. Wing writes:

> The Tao challenges us to see the world as it actually is by accepting the stark truth of the physical laws that control existence and evolution. It challenges us to discover intellectual independence—a state of mind in which we have complete trust in our own perceptions

of the world and can rely fully on the appropriateness of our own inspirations and instincts. It challenges us to find the courage to reject force, and instead to influence others through our example, using nature as our pattern—balancing the extremes in the world instead of causing them.

Wing then adds,

> There are two major changes that occur in the lives of individuals who achieve personal power: the rise of intellectual independence and the need for simplicity.

What is the value of these insights for those seeking to discover how best to thrive in 24/7? Wing's declarations offer three particular lessons. They are as follows:

It is necessary to understand the physical laws of existence. The Tao advocates that we "use nature as our pattern," imitating its workings in all our actions. It defines the laws of nature as a tendency to balance extremes, a bias toward nonresistance, an emphasis on receptivity as well as action. The Tao notes that, after a great storm passes, rigid trees lie snapped upon the ground while flexible bamboo springs quickly back to life. This image instructs us to be flexible, to not resist the world that is evolving around us, but to embrace the changes that come, adapt ourselves to circumstances, *go with the flow.* It also challenges us not to cling to preconceived notions of what we "should" be doing, but take our cues from our world as we observe it in operation.

It is necessary to trust our instincts. Our individual perceptions of the world provide us with the information we need to fine-tune our responses to the events that confront us. Our responses will be appropriate insofar as they come from our deepest core. To exercise influence and shape our lives in a meaningful way, we must therefore know ourselves thoroughly. This will enable us to recognize when our instincts are authentic. We can then trust our responses to suggest the appropriate course of action. And we must honor what we find.

It is necessary to cultivate simplicity. The Tao constantly cautions us that desiring or possessing too many things leads to overattachment, which in turn leads to a loss of independence. If we are too intent upon what we desire, we will add needless complexity to our existence, set ourselves up to make bad decisions, and leave an opening for fear. And so we must constantly ask ourselves how any new acquisition or role might complicate our existence. We must learn not to automatically and unthinkingly equate the notion of progress with that of having, doing, or being *more.*

The lessons of the Tao echo in a *timeless* way many of the *timely* strategies we have explored in this book—Starting at the Core, Locating Your Inner Voice, Getting Comfortable in the Neutral Zone, Integrating Your Passions, Articulating Your Value, Building a Strong Web of Inclusion, Entering into the Economy of the Gift, Connecting with Timeless Rhythms, Cultivating Mindfulness. These are tactics that the ancient Eastern book of wisdom both understands and demonstrates how to support.

Why the overlap?

I believe that the overlap between the strategies outlined in this book and the worldview expressed by the Tao exists because our VUCA environment is characterized by both rapid and constant change. This paradoxically throws us back upon what is eternal and unchanging in human life. And so the mechanical strategies, the emphasis on efficiency and speed, the adherence to rigid patterns and stages of life that typified the industrial era no longer work.

The model has shifted. Our world has become more fluid. And the essence of Eastern wisdom lies in recognizing this fluidity and appreciating its significance.

As Marshall McLuhan, the great futurist, observed back in the 1960s: "Electronic circuitry is Orientalizing the West. The contained, the distinct, the separate—our Western legacy—is being replaced by the flowing, the unified, the fused." The overlap has been apparent to thinkers like McLuhan for several decades. They foresaw networked technology's capacity for eroding barriers. But the impact of that revolution is only now beginning to manifest itself in our everyday lives.

As a result, the structure of our organizations, institutions, communities, and families is becoming less hierarchical, more organic, taking its shape from the technologies we use to do our work. This is why metaphors such as the web are becoming useful to describe how we actually function in the workplace while also serving as blueprints for its evolution.

Working in real time, which today's technology facilitates and indeed demands, forces us to organize our tasks in ways that reflect how life in the universe is also organized. Thus, a comprehension of the timeless physical laws of existence has become more useful than in years past.

The industrial era took its understanding of work from a mechanical model and structured the world of work to accord with that. The knowledge era takes its understanding of work from an organic model and is structuring the world of work to accord with that.

In essence, we are returning to an older model, one that dominated human consciousness before the industrial revolution.

This is the ecology of life in 24/7.

This ecology shapes our responses to our environment. It requires us to move beyond an increasingly obsolete concern with scarcity and recognize the abundance that we confront.

In the industrial era, work and economy depended upon physical commodities that existed in finite supply, as well as upon manufactured goods made from those commodities.

In the knowledge era, work and economy increasingly depend upon human ideas, which are not finite but continue to grow.

Our sense of the infiniteness of knowledge is itself expanding. In seventeenth-century England, for example, it was generally agreed that the poet John Milton *knew everything in the world there was to know.* Today, we all assume that even the most brilliant and learned among us cannot possibly hope to master more than a tiny fraction of the world's knowledge. And we take for granted that the frontiers of knowledge will continue to widen.

We also see that new ways of communicating, new ways of

sharing, transmitting, and attaining knowledge, are expanding with quantum speed. In 1993, fewer than fifty pages were posted on the Internet. In 2001, there are billions.

The dynamic richness of our environment commands our awe and respect. But it also makes it impossible for us to keep up. There is no way that even the most diligent among us can master what comes at each of us every day.

The fact that we cannot keep up paradoxically gives us reason for hope. Since we can never match the pace of change and the development of new forms of knowledge, we are being forced to find other ways. One way lies in recapturing an approach to work and time and effort more like that of the pre-industrial age, while recasting it within the context of abundance.

How might we do this?

Several years ago, I participated in a conference for association executives from all over North America. It was held at a big new hotel in Miami Beach. The event was typical of such gatherings, with people dashing from workshop to general session and back, in rooms darkened to accommodate computer-generated presentations while the glorious Florida sun brightened the beach outside.

It was at this conference that I first heard large numbers of men complaining that work had become so demanding that their lives felt out of balance. I'd heard it from women, of course, but this was something new. Bewilderment and anxiety over this phenomenon seemed now to lie beyond the province of gender. Over lunch, one participant suggested that those who wanted to discuss the topic hold an informal session during the afternoon break.

Despite the lure of the beach, a good number of people

showed up. We swapped familiar stories of overload, discouragement, and exhaustion. But one man held back. He was the director of the Association of Nursery Owners, the members of which own garden centers that grow and sell trees and plants.

Finally, he spoke. He began by acknowledging our stories. He said, "I've got the same problems you do. I have too much work. I travel all the time. I need to spend more time with my family. I do e-mail at midnight. I identify with everything everyone else is saying. And yet, I *know* there's a different way. I know it because I'm around these nursery owners. They don't hurry. You never see them getting frantic. Their meetings are always relaxed. They have this kind of sturdy independence that lets them set their own pace."

What, we wondered, might be their secret?

He responded, "This might sound strange, but I think it comes from working with trees. That'll give you a different perspective about time! Sure, you're busy, you've got orders coming in, you've got suppliers who fail to send the goods they promised and customers who complain that their delivery got screwed up. But if you're used to thinking in terms of twenty or thirty years, which is the time a big pine takes to grow, you're going to think in a different way. You're not going to be in such a hurry. You're going to know there are things you can't control, times when you must surrender. And I think that, ironically, is what gives you strength."

Then he added, "I'm not sure, but I think that's how people *used* to do things. And given the pace today, we can learn from that."

The nursery owners' association director was describing an approach to work common in the pre-industrial era. Tree growers still live in that world, as do farmers. Those of us who love to garden or fish have a glimmer of what it was like, though we rarely bring our perspective and understanding with us to the work we do for pay.

We need to do so.

The speaker in Miami mentioned that the detachment of the nursery owners, along with their acknowledgment of forces that lie beyond their control, gave them a "kind of sturdy independence." And that this independence seemed responsible for their measured pace. The *Tao,* as we saw in the quotes from Wing's translation, also emphasizes intellectual independence, connecting it to an understanding of the physical laws that control our existence.

Obviously, the nursery owners live in harmony with physical laws.

But I believe the lesson we can learn from them goes deeper than that. For it is only by achieving independence that we can manifest the balanced approach that will enable us to thrive in the world of 24/7.

We have stressed many times throughout this book that we are in a strong position to do this because organizations have grown more dependent upon our intelligence and ideas, while we have grown less dependent upon organizations to market and deliver our skills. As Peter Drucker, the philosopher and historian of work, has observed, "The advent of a knowledge economy begins to reverse the traditional balance of power away from organizations and toward individuals."

This is what we must understand if we are to shape our work in our own image and set a pace that allows for real satisfaction. We must know how much and why our talents are needed. We must recognize that we hold the power to sculpt our futures to reflect our needs as they change over time. And we must accept that it lies within our scope to structure our relationships with organizations in ways that meet those changing needs.

Believing it is true is the great challenge of our age. We must know our own power. Everything flows from that.

ABOUT THE AUTHOR

Sally Helgesen is an author, speaker, teacher, and consultant whose specialty is the role of work and leadership in the new economy. She looks at how profound changes in technology, demographics, and business intersect to create unprecedented opportunities for individuals, and how these opportunities are reshaping organizations, institutions, and people's lives.

Her book *The Web of Inclusion: A New Architecture for Building Great Organizations* was hailed in the *Wall Street Journal* as one of the best books on leadership of all time. It explores how innovative organizations can achieve strategic advantage and solve complex problems by making better use of people on the front lines and by forming partnerships. An earlier book, *The Female Advantage: Women's Ways of Leadership,* has been widely hailed as "the classic work" on women's management styles, and is used as a standard text in colleges and universities.

Sally Helgesen has taught seminars at the Harvard Graduate School of Education and at Smith College, and was Visiting Scholar at Northwestern University. She has also consulted for the United Nations, which used her work to create a group of "Centers of Experimentation" that administer programs in developing countries in a decentralized and inclusive way. She is a participant in the Financial Times Knowledge Leadership Dialogue and a member of The Learning Network. She lives in New York City and Chatham, New York.

Sally can be reached via her website at *www.sallyhelgesen.com.*